Beyond Cannery Row

T0385684

Beyond Cannery Row

*Sicilian Women, Immigration, and
Community in Monterey, California,
1915–99*

CAROL LYNN McKIBBEN

University of Illinois Press

URBANA AND CHICAGO

Library of Congress Cataloging-in-Publication Data
McKibben, Carol Lynn, 1955–
Beyond Cannery Row : Sicilian women, immigration, and
community in Monterey, California, 1915–99 / Carol Lynn McKibben.
p.   cm. — (Statue of Liberty–Ellis Island centennial series)
Includes bibliographical references (p.   ) and index.
ISBN-13: 978-0-252-03058-1 (isbn 13 - cloth : alk. paper)
ISBN-10: 0-252-03058-3 (isbn 10 - cloth : alk. paper)
ISBN-13: 978-0-252-07300-7 (isbn 13 - paper : alk. paper)
ISBN-10: 0-252-07300-2 (isbn 10 - paper : alk. paper)
1. Italian American women—California—Monterey—Social
conditions—20th century. 2. Women immigrants—California—
Monterey—Social conditions—20th century. 3. Sicily (Italy)—
Emigration and immigration—History—20th century. 4. Monterey
(Calif.)—Emigration and immigration—History—20th century.
5. Italian American families—California—Monterey—History—20th
century. 6. Fishers—California—Monterey—History—20th century.
7. Fish canneries—California—Monterey—History—20th century.
8. Community life—California—Monterey—History—20th century.
9. Monterey (Calif.)—Social conditions—20th century. 10. Monterey
(Calif.)—Social life and customs—20th century. I. Title. II. Series.
F869.M7M38   2006
305.85'1079476—dc22   2005013682

For Scott, Forever

Contents

Illustrations follow page 12

Acknowledgments

It is a great pleasure to acknowledge the debts I have incurred in writing this book. First, I would like to thank the Sicilian families of Monterey, California, who opened their homes and their hearts to me. They generously allowed me to share their lives as I reconstructed the story of their past. In particular, I am grateful to Peter Cutino, Rosalie Ferrante, Anita Ferrante, and Catherine Cardinale.

I am deeply grateful for the intellectual support, guidance, and wisdom of Mary P. Ryan, who inspired me to begin the process of analyzing this migration experience through a gender-sensitive lens. Jon Gjerde gave me much-needed direction and help as my manuscript evolved through several drafts to incorporate a wider historiography and sources beyond oral histories.

I am grateful to the professional staff at the Bancroft Library, particularly Teresa Salazar, and Dennis Copeland of the California Room at the Monterey Public Library for helping me sift through archives and locate critical documents used in this book.

Steve Baker of the Monterey Institute of International Studies encouraged me to teach courses in International Policy Studies that deepened my understanding of migration processes and required me to take a broad, interdisciplinary, and always global view of migration. Pat Rivette, a supporter of Gender and Women's studies at MIIS and my good friend, helped me with the title of this book.

Friends and colleagues read (sometimes several) draft versions of this manuscript and gave me important criticism, response, and encouragement. I am deeply grateful to every one of them. John Walton provided critical intellectual feedback and insight when I most needed it. Donna Gabaccia, Diane Vecchio, Elliott Barkan, Glenna Matthews, Karen Offen, Ron Bayor, Sally Cole, Linda Reeder, Lydio Tomasi, Kate Davis, Karin Strasser Kauffman, and Susan Shillinglaw each offered very different and equally invaluable perspectives and comments that helped me clarify and sharpen my argument. Diane Belanger, Lila Staples, and Cindy Riebe read and commented on drafts of this manuscript, and always gave me much-needed friendship and encouragement. Sandi Risser, cousin and dear friend, sustained me so many times over the years. Suzanne Desan has given encouragement and support since our graduate school days.

Vicki Ruiz understood and believed in what I was trying to do in this book. I would never have been able to finish it without her. She took time out from her incredibly busy schedule to provide careful readings, critique, response, and support.

Most of all I thank my family. Their love, patience, and confidence always sustained me. My parents, Harry and Geraldine Caliri Copelan, set high expectations with enormous love. I wish they were alive to see the outcome of so many years of intellectual labor. My maternal grandmother, Jenny Paluzzi Caliri, was a model of all things strong and good about Sicilian women. My sister Laurie continues to be my dearest friend and avid supporter. My children, Andrew and Becky, watched me teach, research, and write throughout their entire childhoods. They are my treasures; constant reminders to me of what are most important in life. Finally I thank Scott, my dearest husband, who never wavered in his support and belief in me, whom I love beyond all measure, and to whom I dedicate this book.

Beyond Cannery Row

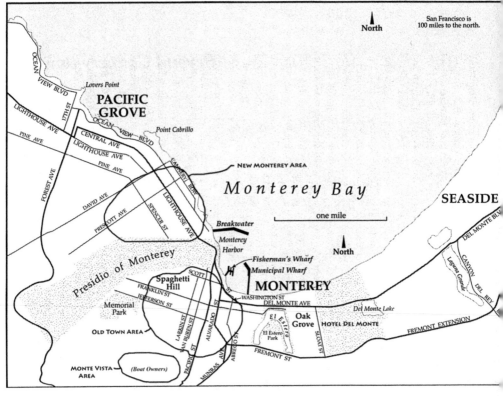

Sicilians expressed class through neighborhood. The wealthiest families lived in the hills, especially on Mar Vista, and the poorest along the wharf. New Monterey was a mixture of ethnicities.

Introduction

We asked for workers but human beings came.
—Max Frisch, 1961

Here is how it was. The families came from Italy for a better life. In
Italy there was nothing. The women couldn't work. There was no
work. Only fishing. That was for the men. So the families got together.
They sent the father or the son first. My grandfather went in 1912. He
went to Chicago, because we had cousins there and he could stay with
them and get on his feet. A lot of men would come and live together
and save up their money to bring the rest of the family over.

    Some women came and some didn't. The women who came, came
because they wanted to keep their families together, not raising them
with the father in America and the mother in Italy. They took a
chance. They were very brave to leave like that. But they wanted to
work, to have a better life, and they couldn't do that in Italy. They
knew there was work for women in America. You could work if you
wanted to. My grandmother worked in a factory in Chicago sewing
pants. My mother went to work in a factory when she was eleven years
old doing piecework. Then, when the uncles moved to Monterey to
fish again, the women all worked in the canneries here [in Monterey].
They did a good job. They didn't bother the government. They raised
their children and their children worked and bought homes. They
took a risk. But it all turned out all right.
—Interview with Nancy Mangiapane, August 3, 1994

The preceding narrative of a Sicilian family migration to Monterey, California,
in 1915 suggests a migration story similar to countless others in late-
nineteenth- and early-twentieth-century America: induced by economics,
negotiated within families, and usually characterized by itinerant factory
labor. However, when Sicilians settled in Monterey they remembered that
they were fishing people, not factory workers. They recalled and reinvented
their identity in a powerful way that fused ethnicity with fishing, and with
Monterey itself.

The re-creation of Sicilian Americans' identity was a deliberate process. Sicilians had to overcome many kinds of differences among themselves and challenges from outsiders in order to accomplish their goal of creating a self-identified ethnic fishing community comfortably situated within the context of modern American life. Sicilian women played a leading role in imagining an identity of Sicilians as ethnic fishers, bringing families together to build a strong community around that identity, and ensuring that the settlement in Monterey was permanent and deeply rooted politically, economically, socially, and culturally.

Sicilian women participated not only in the industrialization of fishing but were also largely responsible for this reinvention of identity as fisherpeople and an adherence to it even without its economic context. Sicilian women expressed their cultural affiliation as fisherpeople in a profound attachment to the landscape of Monterey itself. Their economic, social, and political choices demonstrated how and why this American immigration developed as it did, weaving ethnic identity with a fishing identity.

It is tempting for observers to assume that a community is automatically in place when large numbers of ethnics live in one locale, especially if there is an occupational connection among them. This study of Sicilian migrant fishing people will show that immigrants of a similar ethnicity do not automatically constitute an ethnic community. Rather, ethnicization and community building are step by step, and often arduous, processes. Most important, this story of the migration of Sicilian fisherpeople to Monterey demonstrates that women in ethnic groups must have an active role in creating identity and community in order for migration to become a settlement of people who consider themselves connected along ethnic and occupational lines.

Sicilian migration, both incoming and outgoing, happened continuously throughout the period between 1914 and the present, although not always at the international level, and was made up overwhelmingly of people who considered themselves fishers. Sicilians moved within the triangle of Pittsburg, Martinez, and San Francisco, California, as well as to and from the East and Midwest. Global migration was affected by legislation that restricted flows from time to time, such as in 1924 and during World Wars I and II. Still, the regular, constant migration flow meant that there was no clean break between migration and settlement, or a clear connection between generation and a particular stage of migration. Within families, one spouse might be a third-generation migrant and the other a new migrant. Their children were fourth generation and first generation at the same time. The pattern was repeated in the workplace (on fishing boats and in canneries), and in the context of social gatherings. Even in the present day, Sicilians from Sicily arrive in Monterey and intermarry with Sicilians who are third- or fourth-generation descendants of migrants. Monterey Sicilians return to marry and live in Sicily. The constant migration flow to and from specifically designated villages of fishers has contributed to the conscious formation of a Monterey community of Sicilian fisherpeople that remains relatively and remarkably whole and viable.

Sicilians purposefully reworked themselves from disparate immigrants, originating from different Sicilian fishing villages, and often by way of eastern and midwestern big-city experiences in the United States, as the opening narrative suggested, into one community of Sicilian fishing people. It was neither simple nor straightforward. Still, Sicilian migrants and descendants of migrants felt that communal identity was critical enough that they had to limit assimilation into the broader culture, as well as move beyond village loyalties, personal animosities, and socioeconomic differences to make sure they and their children never lost sight of themselves as one community of Sicilian fisherpeople. "There was always this feeling of continuity, of belonging, as Sicilians and as fishermen," said Elizabeth "Liz" Grammatico, a businesswoman and past president of the Italian Catholic Federation.[1] Yet most Sicilians did not arrive directly from Sicily, and soon enough did not even depend on fishing as their major source of income.

Chronology

This study largely focuses on the period 1920–48, when Monterey's economy seemed to explode, in spite of the global economic Depression, and when Sicilians in particular benefited from the surge of economic growth brought about by the industrialization of sardine fishing. It was during the period 1920 through 1948 that Sicilians migrated to Monterey by the thousands and began a process of intense ethnicization and community building, one shaped, articulated, and made authentic by Sicilian women.[2]

The story of Sicilian Monterey began in the nineteenth century. During the 1880s Monterey had by this time made the transition from Mexican capital to American town. American domination and development of formerly Mexican Monterey culminated during this time.[3] Commercial fishing for whales, abalone, salmon, and a variety of other species played an important role in the local economy throughout the late nineteenth century and into the early years of the twentieth century.[4] Immigrant laborers from Asia and Europe participated actively in catching fish, processing them, and connecting Monterey fisheries into the global marketplace.[5]

The sardine fishing that eventually attracted Sicilian migrants in this study, however, was clearly distinctive from other commercial fishing enterprises in its scope, in the technological change it stimulated, and in the changes it brought to Monterey itself. Sardine fishing burgeoned into a multimillion-dollar industry in the space of a few short years, transformed Monterey into a full-fledged industrialized working-class town, and then ended almost as fast as it began.

Sardine fishing started on a small scale in 1902 with the establishment of one cannery on Fisherman's Wharf. The owner of this cannery, Frank Booth, recruited a young fisheries expert, Norwegian immigrant Knute Hovden, to help him modernize, develop the technology necessary to preserve fish more efficiently, and market his products globally. In 1913 Hovden, in turn, hired a young Sicilian fisherman, Pietro Ferrante, and his brother-in-law Orazio Enea, to organize a labor force of fishermen to focus on sardine fishing. Ferrante and Enea sought fishermen who could be relied upon to bring a steady supply of fish into the cannery.[6]

According to local studies, it was clear to Hovden, Ferrante, Enea, and Booth by the early 1920s that sardine fishing presented an enormous economic opportunity.[7] They were right. The sardine fishing boom went uninterrupted for twenty-eight years. The speedy development of new technologies that allowed for huge catches of sardines also presented a serious processing problem, however. Additionally, the enterprise required the availability of scores of fishermen familiar with the species. Fish needed to be preserved to be marketed. Canneries needed a large, cheap labor force as well as new technology in order to make sardines a profitable commodity. Laborers needed inexpensive places to live that allowed for easy and quick access to the wharf area where fish were processed. However, the labor force needed to be expendable, too. The sardine season only lasted from August until February, and Monterey could not provide attractive, alternative employment for workers year-round. Sicilian immigrants, originally from fishing villages in western Sicily that depended on sardines, among other species, understood that this offered them a perfect economic opportunity.

For boat owners and cannery owners, the prosperity of the sardine years provided opportunities to gain a foothold in Monterey's economy. Women in these families participated actively in driving the family economy toward settlement by purchasing both businesses and real estate. Moreover, they enthusiastically came together to create symbols of ethnicization such as the Santa Rosalia *Festa*, which seamlessly fused fishing with ethnicity and religion.

Working-class Sicilian women worked together on the sardine cannery assembly lines. In the context of the sardine cannery, working-class Sicilian women found common bonds with one another that inspired them to re-create the kind of fishing village identity they remembered from their places of origin in western Sicily. Like their middle-class counterparts, working-class women fused fishing with ethnicization, celebrating everything from family events to community gatherings as a self-identified ethnic fishing community.

It was during this period of intense ethnicization that Sicilians faced hard challenges to their self-concept as a community. In addition to the Sicilians, migrants from the Dust Bowl regions of the United States, and from Japan, Portugal, Yugoslavia, and Spain, eagerly participated in the fishing and canning industry.[8] Mexicans, Californios, and Mexican Americans remained a strong presence in Monterey. Their history and legacy reached back in time for more than two hundred years.[9] The exciting mix of cultures and people may have engulfed Sicilians into the heterogeneity that was Monterey. They had to decide from the moment of settlement if they would preserve their culture as a homogeneous community or assimilate (largely through inter-marriage) into what was becoming a new mainstream of ethnic immigrant people. Sicilians married outsiders almost from the moment of arrival and constantly grappled with the implications of intermarriage.

Sicilian women largely controlled the domestic sphere, which included marriage and family. They coped with intermarriage by resisting it if the marriage in question was to someone considered racially different, such as Asians or Mexicans. In that case the offending family member would be punished with ostracism from the family and emerging community. If the marriage partner could be defined as Spanish rather than Mexican, or was also Catholic, she or he might be incorporated into Sicilian family and community life, requiring conformity and allegiance to Sicilian values and cultural practices.

The most serious challenge to Sicilian efforts to create identity and build community was political. It came with the advent of World War II and the question of allegiance and American identity. The predicament of Sicilian immigrants who did not obtain American citizenship created a climate of fear and uncertainty for Sicilians determined to hold fast to an identity separate from the mainstream. Sicilians assimilated economically into Monterey and American life, but in every other way they remained "a community apart." They resolved the crisis at the time by embracing American citizenship, and by making every effort to demonstrate their collective sense of patriotism and American identity. Nonetheless, the Italian-American Cultural Foundation debated only recently whether to include the word *American* in their designation.

The last successful sardine fishing season, 1948, marked a turning point for the city of Monterey and for Sicilian settlers. The larger community of Monterey turned to tourism after 1948, even reinventing their past through literature to support the concept of their city as a tourist mecca.[10] Cannery Row was transformed, freshened up, and recalled as a cute, quaint reflection of a Steinbeck novel, with all sorts of eccentric, unsavory, but harmless and happy characters.[11] No real but less flamboyant working women and men, with their genuine (rather than caricatured) ethnicity, ethics, or painful labor battles, intervened to complicate the story. The development of the Monterey Bay Aquarium on the site of the original Hovden Cannery epitomized the changeover from a city based on fish as a part of industrial development to one dependent on tourism as its economic foundation, albeit with fish as the main attraction. Local historians depicted the years of industrialized fishing as a mere blip on an economic screen that centered on tourism.

Many Sicilian fisherpeople who had invested in boats and canneries lost everything. Many left the area as a result. Yet most Sicilians stayed, because they had already invested in hotels, restaurants, gift shops, and other businesses that supported the new economics of tourism. Still, Sicilians continued to identify themselves as fisherpeople, even as they turned to other occupations for their livelihoods rather than conform to their collective historical pattern by migrating either for better economic opportunity or to "follow the fish." For Sicilians, fishing in Monterey became a "way of life," a part of who they were, not merely an occupation, like it was for other immigrant participants in fishing, or like the work they did as immigrants in Chicago or Detroit. Fishing in Monterey came to define them as a people in a fundamental way. They identified as fisherpeople for generations.

Historiography

Monterey's history of the migration and settlement of Sicilian fisherpeople is important for what it can help us understand about fishing communities and environment, about women and gender roles, and about the processes of migration in terms of identity formation and reformation, settlement, and community development. It is a specific story about a particular ethnic group, but it has meaning for immigration studies generally. There are several bodies of historical literature that apply to this analysis of the Sicilian fishing migration and community of Monterey. New scholarship on community building suggests that the behavior of Sicilian women in Monterey in the middle decades of the twentieth century was similar to the "porch culture" of working-class American southerners, in which women played critical, even pivotal roles in creating community by supporting one another and acting independently of spouses to accomplish their social, economic, and political goals.[12] Monterey's Sicilian women, however, drew on rather different historical traditions than the women of the rural South.

New scholarship on Sicilian social and cultural life shows that the idea of the passive, reticent Sicilian woman was myth, not reality. Historian Linda Reeder found that the common pattern of male out-migration in Sicily meant that Sicilian women took control of their households and their family lives as a matter of course, routinely working for wages and consistently demonstrating a willingness to challenge authority and wield power in all sorts of ways.[13] The Sicilians who settled Monterey came from this cultural tradition of strong, self-sufficient women, family members of emigrants.

However, the women in Reeder's study were from western Sicily and agricultural regions, the most common study group. Their lives varied from fisherpeople in important ways. Emigration was always a dangerous enterprise with uncertain consequences, but fishing as an occupation meant that emigration was a constant, and dependent not only on changes in environment and the economy, as was agricultural employment. Fishing, all by itself, included an unusual element of danger, which was an aspect not unique to Sicilians, but shared among fishing peoples elsewhere. According to maritime anthropologist John J. Poggie Jr., "Official statistics confirm the extreme risks involved in fishing. Indeed, fishing is far more dangerous in terms of loss of life than coal mining—the most dangerous land based occupation in American society. The Office of Marine Safety in 1972 reported that in 1965 the commercial fisheries of the United States recorded 21.4 deaths per million man-days in contrast to 8.3 in coal mining."[14]

The growing scholarly literature on fisherpeople acknowledges the special role of women as decision makers, actors, and privileged, independent members of families.[15] Anthropologist Sally Cole studied the lives of Portuguese fisherpeople in her work *Women of the Praia,* and highlighted the extent to which women played pivotal roles in family decisions to migrate or not; in the work of fishing and fish processing; and in the creation of community values, behaviors, and mores over time. Anthropologist Marian Binkley also explored women and gender in fishing communities in her study *Set Adrift,* and demonstrated a strong tradition of proactivity and self-sufficiency among women.[16] Sicilians who settled Monterey were accustomed to the power and independence of women in families, both because they came from emigrant Sicilian households and because they came from a long tradition as fisherpeople. As a result, the Sicilians who settled Monterey in the decades prior to 1945 were uniquely poised to create something new, based as much on their special identity as migrant fishers as on their ever-changing identity as Sicilian immigrant Americans. The outcome of the eventual migration of Sicilian fisherpeople to Monterey depended a great deal on what Sicilian women in migrant fishing families decided to do about it.

The new work on immigration by Brettell; Gabaccia and Iacovetta; Glick-Schiller, Basch, and Blanc-Szanton; Hondagneu-Sotelo; and Portes and Rumbaut, among many other scholars, emphasizes the complexities of assimilation, the power of transnational communities in identity formation, and the importance of gender analysis in the process of migration and settlement, from initial decision making to choice of destination site to labor force participation.[17] This new scholarship is almost exclusively focused on the immigration experiences of workers in agriculture and industry, and also usually located in larger population centers. This study shows that fisherpeople are even more likely than other groups to prove new understandings about immigration, and that smaller towns such as Monterey can be just as powerful destination pulls as large cities when it comes to an occupation such as fishing, which in itself is not only a compelling form of identity, but also serves as a strong economic incentive to migrate.

Background and Method

I began my historical analysis of the experience of Sicilian immigrants with the more general assignment of documenting women's work in the fish canneries for a local magazine article I wrote in 1992. The women I originally encountered came from the Dust Bowl, Portugal, Japan, Mexico, Spain, and Sicily. I interviewed them mostly in their homes, and when in homes, always in the kitchen. We talked across so many kitchen tables. I learned about the special camaraderie generated among women who were focused on getting a difficult job done in a harsh work environment: the industrial fish canneries of the 1920s, 1930s, and 1940s. I learned that their work almost, but not quite, bound them into a self-identified interest group of cannery workers. I thought that I would find similarities between fish cannery workers in Monterey and the workers in the fruit canneries of the Santa Clara Valley that Patricia Zavella depicted, and in the women Vicki Ruiz studied in her analysis of cannery workers in southern California.[18]

There were common threads between women fish cannery workers in Monterey and women cannery workers elsewhere. Both groups struggled with the difficulties of balancing household chores with cannery work; the economic frustrations of seasonal labor; the challenges of organizing into unions; and the stresses of recent immigrant experiences, particularly over issues of ethnicity, race and racism, and identity formation. However, though the cannery workers in the Santa Clara Valley and in the Los Angeles area were conscious of ethnic differences, they nonetheless identified primarily as workers. The Monterey fish cannery workers emphasized that they saw themselves separated into two distinct groups: Sicilians and Others. The category of "Other" included immigrants and nonimmigrants. I noticed a general assumption among the women I interviewed for the magazine article that the Sicilians were an exceptional case, with a shared and distinctive story to tell.

As a historian with a special interest in immigration, I found this assumption of difference between Sicilians and everyone else intriguing, mainly because "everyone else" hardly constituted a homogeneous group. Rather, fish cannery workers were a disparate mixture of nationalities and ethnicities, constructed and reconstructed over time.[19] As the granddaughter of Sicilian immigrants myself, and the niece of a fisher family, I was both curious and determined to understand what being Sicilian meant, and why it seemed so powerful, overriding "worker" as an identity marker in the Monterey context.

I used the method of snowball sampling to conduct my oral history research. I originally made several futile attempts to contact local Sicilians and interview them as part of an oral history project that would become my doctoral dissertation. I met with more resistance than cooperation, until my mother and aunt intervened. I needed to be considered part of the community in order to access personal family histories, and only my mother's and aunt's explicit endorsements accomplished that. They called relatives, friends, and acquaintances and connected me to the people who would become my original narrators. Those people, in turn, introduced me to others. I attended community events organized by the local Italian Catholic Federation. I participated in small gatherings of women's groups, and visited several generations of each family I interviewed. I tried, as much as possible, to interview people one on one, both because it was easier to record their stories and because it was more comfortable than if they were interviewed in couples or in groups.

I drew informants for my interviews equally among migrants from the three major villages of origin in Sicily: Isola Della Femina, San Vito Lo Capo, and Marettimo, all located on the northwestern coast of Sicily between the urban centers of Palermo and Trapani. I spent one spring and summer (1998) doing fieldwork and interviews in Sicily in the three villages of origin.

I collected oral histories for eight years. I interviewed 150 people in depth: 100 women and 50 men. They were chosen at random, but self-selected as well; those connected to my mother and aunt went first, followed by individuals who were particularly active, involved members of the community. Sicilians who remained active in community events were more likely to articulate their own identity as Monterey Sicilians and also more apt to emphasize the strength and continuity of Sicilian communal life than other, less-involved immigrants and descendants of immigrants.

About half of the participants in the interviews were from working-class backgrounds. I defined working class as people who worked either in the canneries or on fishing boats but did not own either, although home ownership was common among all classes. Working-class people often had extended kin connections with people who did own canneries and fishing boats, so there was not a rigid divide within given extended family groups. Indeed, a given extended family group often included a variety of cousins and distant relatives of different classes.

I interviewed people of different generations, and at different stages of migration order to get as full a picture as possible of the migration and settlement of Sicilian Monterey. Still, oral history involves memory and perception on the part of individuals now removed from the moments they described to me. Yet the voices in this book shed an important light on the history and development of an ethnic immigrant fishing community. The narrative examples I used in this work were chosen based on the extent that I found them to be both representative of the community as a whole and especially vivid in description, expression, and recall. I tried to include as many different voices as possible.

I balanced Sicilian voices with a series of four interviews with six women who identified themselves as Spanish, four interviews with six Portuguese women, and four with Japanese women. These interviews were particularly helpful in my understanding of the social and cultural worlds of the canneries and of the variations in which other ethnic immigrants to Monterey expressed identity, especially through ethnic festivals.

I utilized the narratives to form my own analysis of the history of community development among Monterey's Sicilian fishers. This is not a collection of oral histories so much as it is an analysis of community building among Sicilian fisherpeople, one that uses narrative accounts as a significant historical resource. I was a privileged listener as well as a scholar. As such, I was careful to preserve the privacy and identities of the narrators. All narrators were given the choice to use pseudonyms, which I noted throughout the text. Their stories are treasures, and I did not want to expose or offend in my analysis of them.

I balanced the oral interviews with newspaper accounts from the *Monterey Peninsula Herald* and from records in special collections in the Bancroft Library, the Monterey Museum of History, and the California History Room in the Monterey Public Library in order to discover the public history of Sicilians in Monterey and to add other perspectives to the personal views of the past that oral histories gave. I analyzed the manuscript censuses for 1880, 1900, 1910, and 1920. I analyzed the tax assessors' records of property ownership for Monterey County from 1914 through 1960, as well as city directories for evidence of Sicilian property ownership and investment compared to other immigrant groups. I conducted a random sample of marriage licenses issued between 1909 and 1979 for empirical evidence of rates of intermarriage and persistence of community.

This story begins with an overview of the historical context of Sicilian migrants. I analyzed both the literature on the nature of fishing communities and the scholarship on Italian migration to help explain why and how initial migration decisions were made, the early goals and strategies of migrant families, patterns of settlement, and finally the importance of Monterey as an eventual destination point.

Chapter 2 focuses on the workplace, particularly on the fish cannery. Unlike the all-male fishing boat, which was a discrete entity of family and kin group, the cannery was a site of interaction with Sicilians of other kin and family groups and of other villages, as well as migrants from other parts of Italy, Europe, Asia, Mexico, South America, and the United States. Sicilian women had the opportunity to make money for themselves and to make connections to the environment of American Monterey through cannery work, like so many other women who worked in canneries.[20] This gave them a new sense of worldliness and independence, which they expressed by making rather bold financial decisions for themselves and their families. Their economic choices had the effect of ultimately changing the course of the collective ethnic pattern of migration.

Chapter 3 examines family life and family relationships. Women managed family life as they negotiated with the men in their lives. They also maneuvered either to alter or to hold onto positions of power among themselves. The conflicts that ensued from those efforts demonstrated just how an ethnic group evolved along class lines. Women represented class for their entire family. Women's behavior often determined how whole families landed on the socioeconomic scale and also whether the entire family would settle permanently in Monterey. The most successful stayed. More than any other indicator, family relationships and gender roles demonstrated just how important women were to the outcome of migration and settlement.

Chapter 4 concentrates on the issue of citizenship and ethnicity as Sicilians were required to come to terms with identity in the chaos and confusion surrounding United States policy on "enemy aliens" during World War II. They responded in gendered ways to the crisis and the challenges that came with it. Women redefined themselves in the wake of accusations of disloyalty during the war's early years. They became citizens in large numbers, supported family donations of money to the war effort, relaxed previously strict family boundaries on intermarriage, and allowed themselves to be held up as martyrs when sons died in the fighting. They moved, as much as possible, into the mainstream of American patriotic life. However, men, especially those from elite families, played a more active role in moving the Sicilian community into a redefinition of themselves as American citizens. They successfully drew media attention to their patriotic activities and maintained a central role in the sardine industry. They involved themselves in politics at the local level.

Chapter 5 examines the role of ritual activity in Sicilian life and how public rituals inspired and activated by women served to heal the wounds inflicted by the experience of relocations during the war years. Sicilian women expanded prayer groups into larger public celebrations in order to overcome all sorts of internal ethnic boundaries, especially those of class, and also to link their ethnic community to the broader culture of Monterey. The leadership and participation of Sicilian women in public ritual demonstrated their acute awareness of the importance of transforming their own community into an ethnic enclave of fisherpeople, and infusing the city of Monterey with their own sense of identity, culture, and history. In this way, Monterey absorbed Sicilian culture just as much as Sicilians absorbed the mainstream.

Monterey as a city remains conspicuously connected not just to its industrialized fishing past, but to the specific culture of Sicilian fishing villages. Although sardine fishing ended, Sicilians continue to hold an important economic, social, and political stake in the life of the city, which is unique among the various ethnic groups that settled in Monterey. The Conclusion of this study examines this phenomenon and its implications for a fuller scholarly understanding of immigration and identity formation as a gendered process.

Sicilian fishing women at work, 1932. Author's collection.

Sicilian men mending nets in the early years of settlement. Courtesy of the California History Room Archives, Monterey Public Library.

The earliest years on the cannery assembly line, 1930. Author's collection.

Floor lady on the cannery assembly line, 1940s. Courtesy of the California History Room Archives, Monterey Public Library.

Taking the oath of citizenship, 1945. Courtesy of Joe and Catherine Cardinale.

Boat owners' formal dinner banquet, 1948. Courtesy of Joe and Catherine Cardinale.

Bride just coming out of San Carlos Church. Courtesy of the California History Room Archives, Monterey Public Library.

Barbecue on the wharf, Santa Rosalia, 1960s. Courtesy of the California History Room Archives, Monterey Public Library.

Santa Rosalia parade, angels, and float, 1950s. Courtesy of the California History Room Archives, Monterey Public Library.

1. Sicilian Women, Fishing Lives, and Migration Strategies

> I went to America to work, but when I arrived there, the thought of my family, my wife, my son, was always in my head. Do I return or do I stay? Without my wife I did not know how to orient myself.
> —Interview with Joseph Deangelini (pseudonym), March 2, 1994

> In the old times, this community was kept alive by matriarchy . . . women would sow the grain. They would gather wood and take care of the vegetable gardens while the men were fishing . . . the woman from Marettimo has been able to gain independence and authority thanks to her ability to manage the family, and help the husband with the equipment for fishing.
> —Leonarda Vaccaro, "Marettimo and Monterey: Two Communities in Comparison" (1995)

> When you are a fisherman, it's in your blood. You have to fish. You have to follow the fish. You have to be at sea. It's a way of life. That's what I used to tell the children when they would complain about [their father] being gone so much. "This is our way of life," I would tell them.
> —Interview with Catherine Cardinale, September 7, 1994

The chapter begins with an analysis of the demographics of the Sicilian migration over time to demonstrate that it was clearly a family and chain migration from the outset. Next, this chapter will explore the ways in which the Sicilian migration to Monterey conforms to new scholarly understandings of migrant fisherpeople generally, particularly with regard to the roles of women.

Demographics and Population Flows

Sicilian migrants to Monterey originated mainly from only thirty-five family groups. The oral histories indicated that they came to North America in three distinct waves, beginning around 1880. According to census records they did not settle in Monterey until 1915. Monterey had a population of only 2,583 in 1880, which included only three Italian families, none of whom were Sicilian.[1] They identified themselves as Swiss-Italian. The census also showed three Italian men who lived alone, and three women and twelve children, all of whom lived with male heads of households. None of the Italians in the 1880 census listed fishing as an occupation, and only one owned his home.[2]

The demographic context of the rest of Monterey at 1880 was predominantly Mexican American. This designation signified a constructed identity that was constantly evolving to include Native Americans, Mexican immigrants, and Americans from the Southwest, East, and Midwest.[3] The vast majority of the population declared themselves native Californians and also claimed California as the birthplace of their parents. It cannot be emphasized strongly enough that Monterey in 1880 was a town of native borns, a place where the descendants of Mexican-Indian-Spanish and Americans lived in the majority, and where European and Asian immigrants formed a small part of the population.[4]

The European immigrant population included a mixture of Yugoslavians, Scandinavians, Irish, Portuguese (originating from the Azores and migrating by way of Hawaii), Chinese, and Japanese. The Portuguese lived mainly on dairy farms on the outskirts of Monterey and in Carmel Valley in large family groups that included an average of six to eight children. Chinese migrants were mostly single males who lived in groups of fifteen or more. Japanese migrants included large groups of males too, but also many young families with children. Scandinavians and Irish lived in nuclear family groups. Occupations were varied, but fishing was rarely mentioned as an occupation by anyone. Immigrants were usually identified as "merchant," "bar-owner," or "farmer" at one end of the class structure, and "laborer" or "helper" at the other.[5]

The first wave of Sicilian fishing migrants came mainly from the villages of Isola Della Femina and San Vito Lo Capo. First-wave migrants to Monterey left Sicily to follow the fish to North Africa before coming to the United States. Once in America, families lived in the East and worked in industrial centers. Many of Monterey's Sicilian immigrants located their place of birth as Michigan, New York, or Illinois. Those who eventually settled in Monterey also came by way of Pittsburg, Martinez, or San Francisco, California.[6]

By 1900 things began to change for Monterey, both economically and socially. The Southern Pacific Railroad and the Del Monte Hotel, which had been established in 1880, brought investment capital into the old city (now reincorporated). Tourists played golf at the new golf course, toured Seventeen

Mile Drive along the coast, or attended the racetrack and polo field, creating a gentrified elite. Most important, the city of Monterey itself altered when a new city engineer designed streets and neighborhoods, an attempt to conform to a Progressive Era idea of an American town, rather than accepting the more chaotic and interesting mix of houses and neighborhoods typical of nineteenth century Mexican American society. An artist colony emerged. Businessmen invested in shops and restaurants. The Presidio was reactivated as an American military base.[7]

The population of Monterey increased to 5,355, but the resident population remained similar in makeup to that of 1880.[8] While Scandinavians, Portuguese, Japanese, and Chinese continued to be significant minorities, Italians appeared negligible in the census. There were only two Italian families listed in the 1900 census, with eight children between them. None of the seven Italian adults listed in the 1900 census came from Sicily. They specified their origins as Swiss-Italian, French-Italian, or German Italian, suggesting northern rather than southern Italian origins. As for occupation, the landowners called themselves farmers or horticulturists. Those who were poorer were "laborers" or "wood-cutters." No one listed his occupation as fisherman, although this is not to suggest no one actually fished for a living.

There was a slight increase in the Italian population by 1910, although the population of Monterey remained stable. The Italians listed themselves in the census as Swiss-Italian, German-Italian, or French-Italian, still indicating a northern Italian rather than a southern Italian migration. Of the thirty-six Italian adults in this census, five were women, all of whom lived with male heads of households. They had fifteen children between them. Eight households were male only. None of the Italians in the 1910 census listed "fishing" as an occupation. The Italians who lived in Monterey in 1910 still identified their occupations as "farmers," "horticulturists," or "laborers." The immigrant population in Monterey in 1910 was overwhelmingly Portuguese, Japanese, and Chinese.[9] The Japanese dominated fishing on the small scale that it was until 1910.[10]

The 1915 tax assessors' records show a shift in demographics beginning in 1914.[11] Beginning in 1914, Italian surnames began to appear in the tax records. By 1915 those Italian names were familiar as belonging to the earliest migrants from fishing families. Ferrante, Enea, Lucido, Russo, and Buffo joined the list of Gallo, Giannini, and Giusseppi that appeared before 1914.

According to narrative accounts, between 3,000 and 4,000 Sicilians made their way to Monterey to fish for sardines, salmon, and other varieties of fish from 1880 to 1914.[12] This was a huge number of people, considering that the population of Monterey was only about 5,000 at 1900, and the population of the whole county of Monterey was only 11,300 by 1910.[13] The census data does not record such an influx. It is unlikely that Sicilians actually lived in Monterey in the numbers they claimed in the oral interviews, although it is probable that there were more migrants than the census accounted for. These were people on the move and difficult to keep track of as they traveled back and forth to Pittsburg, San Francisco, and Martinez as well as to Detroit, Chicago, Milwaukee, and the home villages in Sicily.

The advent of World War I and the restrictive immigration policies of the 1920s, such as the 1921 Quota Act and the 1924 Immigration Act, ended the flow of this first big migration, although there continued to be considerable movement between Monterey and the Pittsburg-Martinez area and also between San Francisco and the smaller towns. Families were cut off from travel to and from Sicily, just as the industrialization process began to revolutionize sardine fishing. Monterey looked increasingly attractive as a year-round residence, especially during the war years, as it became clear that the need for labor on the boats and in the new canneries might be a good economic strategy for families eager to acquire property and pursue upward mobility.

A second wave of migration to Monterey began in the mid-1920s, not necessarily directly from Sicily but by way of San Francisco, Pittsburg, or Martinez. This wave conformed to census data, which showed inflows of migrants who claimed in 1920 that their country of origin was Italy but who may have lived in various parts of the United States for some time before that.[14] According to the oral histories, almost all of these migrants had kin and village ties to the first settlers. They came because word spread that Monterey was an ideal location for fisherpeople. Mike Maiorana recalled, "We saw guys making money who couldn't even put two shoelaces together [in Sicily]. We thought, 'Hey, if that guy can do it, think about what I can do.'"[15] Frances Archdeacon, a resident of Martinez, California, remembered hearing stories from her uncles that the fish were so plentiful in Monterey that they "are coming into the houses."[16] Women were as interested as men were in the work opportunities being offered. The census supported the oral histories in terms of sex ratios in 1920. However, though the oral histories emphasized that many migrants of both sexes came as young, single people, the census showed the predominance of families. Both may have been true. Young people of either sex would not have been allowed to live alone, and most likely arrived accompanied by parents or extended family.

It is difficult to exaggerate the tremendous physical and demographic change that took place in Monterey by 1920. By 1920 the wharf and downtown area had completely transformed into a noisy collection of peoples from all over southern Europe and Asia. The fishing industry, with its sights, sounds, and smells of fish being caught and processed, gave Monterey the distinctive aura of working-class fisherpeople. The wharf area of Cannery Row was "alive and bustling" with the energy of the immigrant working classes who sought to take advantage of plentiful sea life. Upper Franklin Street, Van Buren Street, Larkin Street, Watson Street, Scott Street—all former residences of native-born Californios were nicknamed Garlic Hill and Spaghetti Hill by the 1920s to reflect the influx of Sicilian people who now lived there. The neighborhoods of New Monterey were more of a mixture of Spanish, Mexican, Portuguese, Japanese, and Sicilian workers.[17]

The 1920 census showed a population in Monterey of 6,680, with significant numbers of immigrants from Italy and southern Europe.[18] The population of Portuguese and Spanish residents increased significantly. Portuguese women and men often listed the Azores as their original home. Many came from farming rather than fishing backgrounds and shifted from whaling to dairy farming over the course of the early twentieth century. Large numbers of Japanese families had moved into the area along the wharf. Many Japanese women and men listed their occupations as fishermen and fish cutters. The Chinese population remained considerable and consisted of many families, rather than predominantly male only.

The census of 1920 showed the first significant presence of Italian fisherpeople. There were 972 Italians. The Italians in this census lived along the wharf and downtown area, and overwhelmingly declared that they were fishermen by occupation. Most of their surnames are familiar as belonging to the Italian families who traced their origins to the three Sicilian villages and families identified in the oral histories. Of the 972 Italians listed in the census, 275 were male, 218 were female, and 479 were children age sixteen years or younger. Many families included lodgers or boarders, but these tended to be closely related to either the adult male or adult female head of household. There were only a handful of households with large numbers of single men living together, and even these seldom included more than six to eight men (unlike the twenty or thirty single men who made up households of Chinese migrant laborers in Monterey). The vast majority of Sicilians in Monterey are listed in the census in nuclear family or extended family groups, which consisted of parents, children, and perhaps a grandparent or adult sibling of the household heads.

The census was useful in showing a clear starting point (1920) for the settlement of people to Monterey who identified both as fisherpeople and Sicilians. It was also critical in showing the migrants generally to be young people of both sexes who lived in nuclear family groups, occasionally sharing their dwellings with a close relative or two (i.e., a parent or adult sibling). The census records missed the period when sojourning males may have come first, lived in boardinghouses, and only sent for families after they had established homes and livelihoods, but the oral histories suggested this was the common pattern. The population of Monterey reached 9,141 in 1930 and 10,084 by 1940. Approximately one-third of this population was Sicilian in origin.[19]

A third wave of migrants arrived in the late 1940s, in the postwar years. Manuscript census data are not available for this last group, but tax assessors' records showed significant increases in home ownership for families with Sicilian surnames who claimed to have been part of this third wave.[20] As with the first two groups, they tended to be young people of marriageable age, of both sexes, who were tempted by the success of fellow villagers. Many more of this third wave claimed their place of origin as the island of Marettimo than San Vito Lo Capo or Isola Della Femina. The tax assessors' records confirmed that the migration in the 1940s was predominantly of Marettimares.[21]

Fishing Culture

Monterey Sicilians came from a tradition of fishing people originally, whatever their interim experiences as American immigrants. As such, they shared a historical understanding of gender that valued women as decision makers, workers, and as the very foundation of their respective families and communities. Many cultures attribute power to women, particularly as mothers, but the peculiar lives of fisherpeople meant that female power was taken to a new level.

The new scholarly literature that focuses on the lives of fishing peoples comes largely from the field of marine anthropology. While environmental scientists and economists have been deeply concerned about marine ecosystems and fisheries management, they nonetheless make little effort to understand the human populations, the fishing peoples, who are intimately involved in the very fisheries that scholars and policy makers are trying to protect. According to marine anthropologist James McGoodwin, "Heretofore, the stress has been on conservationist/biologist concerns, or economic concerns, or a combination of the two. But fisheries experts are coming to pay attention to fishers and fishing peoples, as they should."[22] Furthermore, he argued, "At the most fundamental level . . . fisheries are a *human* phenomenon, since there can be no fishery without human fishing effort."[23] Mc-

Goodwin urged scholars and policy makers at all levels to work harder to achieve better understandings of the human communities that sometimes appear to behave against their own economic and ecological self-interest, but who have much to contribute to marine policy, particularly with regard to conservation.

As McGoodwin suggests, the scholarly debates on fisheries and marine policy center largely on the role fishing peoples ought or ought not to play in terms of management of an increasingly scarce resource. However, there is a general consensus among scholars that the social organizations of fishing communities share certain common characteristics, the most important one being the role of women. Studies spanning eras and cultures, from nineteenth-century Portuguese fisherpeople to twentieth-century Texas shrimpers and New England cod fishing communities, to the fisherpeople of Mexico, Peru, Nova Scotia, Greenland, Norway, Newfoundland, and on the coasts of Africa and Asia, demonstrate drastic cultural differences. In spite of these variations, fisherpeople share this one commonality of social organization in which women were left to fend for themselves for weeks and months, even for years at a time while men went to sea. Women fisherpeople tended to develop a sense of independence, which often contrasted sharply with other women in their class, culture, or national group.[24]

Cross-culturally, women adapted to long stretches of time spent away from partners by becoming actors in a way that was unusual, especially for married women, until very recently. Important decisions often had to be made, and were made, without the participation of males in the household. Fishing environments are, and were, overwhelmingly female spaces. Males come and go, as they pursue livelihoods following migrant fish. McGoodwin summed up the scholarly consensus as follows: "The life situations of fishermen's wives and their central role in the economic and social affairs of their communities contribute importantly to the distinctive character of fishing cultures . . . [and] many fishing communities manifest tendencies toward matriarchy and matrifocality." He concluded that women were vital to fishing communities, "the mainstay" not only of home, family, and social life, but also in "local economic affairs. . . . Men are so often away and the women must take on proportionally more responsibility in the community, [so] it is no surprise that fishermen's wives are often more independent and are accorded relatively greater prestige in fishing communities than the women in non-fishing families. This phenomenon has been reported in such disparate regions as south India, West Africa, New England, Great Britain, Taiwan, and Japan." Furthermore, he argued, "discussion of the vital role of women in fishing communities is probably the greatest lacuna in the available literature on fishers," one that is only "slowly being addressed."[25]

Robert Lee Maril, a marine anthropologist who examined the lives of shrimp fishers in Texas in his work *Texas Shrimpers: Community, Capitalism, and the Sea,* conducted extensive interviews with families over several generations and concluded that "during her husband's absence, the shrimper's wife is both mother and father for her family. This means she must not only carry out the traditional role of housewife but must also respond to the daily demands that her husband would handle. A shrimper expects his wife to cope with emergencies on her own. His wife was liberated long before the feminist movement. He was proud that his wife could mow the lawn, do minor repairs on the car, and pay the bills—all traditional male roles."[26]

One Sicilian scholar, Leonarda Vaccaro, used the term "little matriarchies" to describe the fishing villages under study here. She conducted oral interviews with villagers from Marettimo to demonstrate gender roles in social organization. "We created our own little group you know. The wives of all the men that had emigrated united, they saw each other 'Did you receive any letter from your husband? And what does he say? Nothing, they work, they go out with their boat and they cannot complain about the catch. They became very close and they confided in saying my husband sent me 2,000 liras or 10,000 liras. When they sent money with a letter it was a celebration,' explained Paolina Mineo."[27]

The Sicilians I interviewed for this project, on both sides of the ocean, resoundingly supported the new scholarly literature on fisherpeople that places fisherwomen at the very heart of families. Family migration decisions depended on the adults of both sexes, but the oral histories emphatically stressed the role of women as vital to all decision making in families, especially about what exactly constituted "home": "The families were almost matriarchal. When the women said it was time to move, we moved," said Theresa Sollazzo.[28] "In the Italian family, women have a way of running things. My mother was the brain of the family. She made all the decisions. [She] really dominated my decision process," explained Mike Maiorana in reference to his family's choice to migrate to Monterey.[29] Anita Ferrante remembered a visit to Sicily with her parents taken a few years after the family migrated to Monterey. The family had prospered in Monterey, but had not formally decided on a permanent home. At one point during the visit, Anita's father turned to her mother and asked, "What are we going to do? What is your decision? Where do you want to live?" Her mother answered that she wanted to go home: "My home is Monterey." The family did not consider the question again.[30]

In studies of fisherpeople generally, women in fishing families rarely followed men in migration. Instead, they pursued strategies that allowed for more independent lives at home.[31] This happened in the villages under study here as well. It is important to remember that not all families joined in the migration to Monterey. When women in families refused to participate, men either returned to Sicily or separated permanently from their families. Antoinette Corbello (pseudonym) explained her family history: "My grandmother refused to come [to the United States] because of her health. Her two daughters stayed with her. After she got very sick, my grandfather returned [to Sicily] to help take care of her. Then she died. Then my grandfather came to Monterey with my aunts [the two daughters]."[32] In this family, the grandmother exercised clear choice, and decided against migration, regardless of her husband's decision to settle permanently in Monterey. Her daughters may have wanted to migrate but postponed their own migration in order to do the best thing for the family, which, in this case, meant caring for their mother. They left only after their mother's death.

Maria Mineo remembered longing for a father who remained separated from her and her brother for many years. The children were reared by grandparents in Sicily. Mrs. Mineo's mother wanted to migrate but "couldn't leave her parents. They were very old. Then my mother died [in childbirth] before we could all go to be with my father." Her father remarried and started a second family in San Francisco. It was not until Mrs. Mineo was a teenager that she was able to migrate to the Bay Area to join her father and stepmother. Mrs. Mineo did not get along with her stepmother and moved to Monterey to live with an aunt and uncle. Her birth mother had chosen parents over husband. She had expected to join her husband in San Francisco at some point after her parents died. She died first.[33]

It often took hard evidence of prosperity abroad to convince many women to give up their lives in their home villages for a new life in an unknown environment. "The husband had to convince her that Monterey was a good place, good weather, friendly people, easy to make a living," explained Hope Cardinalli.[34] Theresa Sollazzo agreed. "The only way my mother would come was that she knew my father had a job and a home for her and us. The main thing was she wanted a father in the family. But she was afraid. She had to have security."[35]

Fisherpeople share another important characteristic, which also cuts across time spans, cultures, and geography. That is, they depend economically on

a fragile resource: wild fish populations. Inevitably, fisherpeople face depletion or, at least, moments of scarcity from overfishing, changes in water
temperatures or climate, or fish life cycles and migratory patterns, about
which much is still not known or understood by science.

Increasingly, marine anthropologists have prompted environmentalists
to study the relationship between communities of humans and the communities of fish that humans depend upon for their livelihoods.[36] The two
kinds of communities share a symbiotic relationship; they cannot really be
understood apart from one another. Sometimes a declining fish population
results in a declining human population. Sometimes the human population
(the fishermen at least) migrate temporarily as a result of depleted fish resources. Fishermen often worked part time in land-based occupations to
supplement their incomes. It was rare, however, for fisherpeople to change
employment completely, much less their identity, simply because their local
fish population either migrated or was depleted. Fishing is not something
one does; it is something one is. It is "in the blood," as Sicilians would say.
Studies of New Jersey fishers concluded that "Fishermen derive a considerable 'satisfaction bonus' from their work. Fishing is not merely a means to
an end, but is intrinsically rewarding. . . . Fishing is not just a livelihood, it
is a way of life."[37]

Historical Context

Monterey's Sicilians conformed to this general pattern of fisherpeople in
their native Sicily. Economically, they depended on fishing for their livelihoods and identified as fisherpeople. When fishing became untenable economically, they either emigrated or sought land-based extra work to get by.
However, they did not stop thinking of themselves as fishers. Many immigrant
Sicilians in Monterey, or their elders, remembered an environment in Sicily
teeming with fish, but one that had become seriously depleted in the early
years of the twentieth century. Giuseppe Febbraio, an elderly man from
Marettimo, recalled, "When I was six years old, I started being a fisherman.
Then you could catch the fish with a '*coppo*' [a stick with a little net at the
end]. There was so much fish . . . sardines, mackerel, anchovies, also red mul-
lets, scorpion fish, and groupers. . . . Now, when you catch one, you must
make a sign of the cross."[38]

Giuseppe Spadaro, age eighty-six, recalled his father's experience: "The
sardines were so many that the whole quay was full . . . my father had 120
kilos of sardines, but the salt owner had finished, so he was obliged to throw

all the fish on the ground for the people to use for manure." By the time Mr. Spadaro came of age, however, the sardines were so depleted that he immigrated to Monterey to continue pursuing his livelihood as a sardine fisherman.[39]

Migration—at least temporary migration—was a common response to scarcity on the part of fishing people. However, the usual pattern cross-culturally was for fishermen to migrate, while fisherwomen stayed behind to maintain home and family. What was unique about Sicilian female migration among Sicilian fisherpeople in Monterey was the extent to which women participated in these migrant streams rather than continue to remain behind in Sicily in communities socially organized around female presence and male absence. This pattern conforms more closely to scholarly literature on Italian female migrants who chose migration as men did, for economic and social goals of their own—sometimes to improve their marital prospects, often to enhance their economic opportunities.[40] Still, few people migrated entirely without family consensus, whether they were male or female. According to Donna Gabaccia and Franca Iacovetta in a recent collection of scholarly work on Italian migration, "All the evidence . . . suggests that decisions about which family members would migrate and which remain at home reflected shrewd calculations about work opportunities—in both subsistence production and for wages—at home and abroad and for both men and women . . . studies that focus exclusively on Italy's male migrants have helped to generate wrongheaded generalizations."[41]

New scholarship has rectified our understanding of migration, and also emphasized that it was, and is, a complex process that must be viewed from many different angles, including perspectives of female migrants.[42] John Bodnar, Caroline B. Brettell, Nancy Foner, Suzanne Sinke, and other feminist historians have emphasized the central, critical experience of women in the migration process.[43] They studied women's experiences not in isolation from men's but rather in the whole context of family migration experiences. Nancy Foner argued in her study *New Immigrants in New York,* "Because in their roles as women they are intimately involved with men, the lives of all migrants are likely to be affected by changes in the status of women."[44]

Alejandro Portes emphasized gender and the household as key categories of analysis that "like class and race . . . represent a master dimension of social structure [that] can yield novel insights into many phenomena."[45] John Bodnar agreed. In a sweeping analysis of nineteenth- and twentieth-century migration to the United States, he argued that "families and households were the predominant form in which all immigrants entered the industrial-urban

economy and ordered their lives."[46] Nancy Foner examined family and migration in separate studies of Jamaican and Vietnamese migrants to New
York. Immigrants, she argued, do not live as isolated individuals, but "live
out much of their lives in the context of families."[47]

Patricia R. Pessar and Sherri Grasmuck made a compelling case for the
importance of gender and household analysis in their study of the migration
experiences of Dominicans to and from New York between 1965 and 1981:
"The household is the social unit [whose members] make decisions about
whether migration will occur, who will migrate, and whether migration will
be temporary or permanent. These decisions . . . are guided by kinship and
gender ideologies as well as by hierarchies of power within households."[48]
Analysis of gender and household become even more significant when as-
sessing out-migration or return migration, according to Pessar and Grasmuck: "We must recognize that it is not individuals but households that
mobilize resources and support, receive, and allocate remittances, and make
decisions about members' production, consumption, and distribution activities. . . . [A]n understanding of who remains behind in migrant households and what these persons' relations are to other migrant and nonmigrant
households is essential to an assessment of the costs and benefits of out-
migration for distinct social class in sending communities."[49]

Thus, gender analysis increasingly informs the new scholarship on fishing
peoples, the newest work on immigration generally, and the newest scholarship on Italian immigration—with good reason. Women were central players in fishing communities and in migration streams, and were critical actors
in families, especially so in migrant Sicilian families.[50] These threads of historical scholarship and cultural context demonstrate why a fishing community, with all its peculiarities, evolved in Monterey among Sicilian immigrants, as well as why Sicilian women were the crucial players in inventing
and forming that community.

Sicily in Historical Context

I visited the northwestern coast of Sicily in the spring and summer of 1998.
My goal was to get a better sense of this particular fishing region in order to
understand the points of origin for Monterey's Sicilian families and also the
extent to which the points of origin had, in the decades of the 1980s and
1990s, become return migrations. I wanted to get a feel for the landscape,
both the natural and human environment of the Sicilian villages of fisherpeople that made them different from fisherpeople elsewhere.

I was struck immediately that the villages were small, tightly woven enclaves. Residents of these villages share surnames and strong physical resemblances to their counterparts in Monterey. I encountered several Californians also visiting Sicily whom I had already interviewed in Monterey. I met several American women in their thirties whose grandparents once migrated to Monterey but who themselves returned to the village of origin to marry and raise children.

The villages were concentrated spaces, hugging the water. Almost everyone has a view of the sea. Homes remain tiny and unobtrusive on the outside but hidden from public view, and they were spacious, with many rooms in comfortable, if not lavish, surroundings. People expressed class differences on the inside, rather than on the outside, of their residences in the villages, although the wealthier families of San Vito Lo Capo tended to live on the outskirts of town rather than on the waterfront. In Marettimo, however, the most humble-looking waterfront dwelling might hide an enormous home filled with contemporary furniture.

It took me forty-five minutes to walk through the entirety of the village of San Vito Lo Capo, and less than thirty minutes to traverse the entire populated area of Marettimo. On the way, I felt as though I encountered everyone, and that everyone knew exactly who I was and what I was doing there. I made arrangements in advance of coming, but it was a great surprise to me that I was so well known so quickly, within a day of arriving, in spite of the fact that it was the tourist season and the villages were also crowded with visitors from northern Italy and western Europe, particularly Germany.

By the time of my visit, it was clear that while the villagers had not stopped thinking of themselves as fisherpeople, nor had they completely stopped fishing, they had transformed their economy exactly the way the Sicilians of Monterey had. They had become restaurateurs, hotel owners, part of a burgeoning tourist industry. Economic development on one side of the ocean paralleled development on the other.

The people of Sicily were able to accomplish this for precisely the same reason the people of Monterey found tourism so profitable. They lived in an area of incredible natural beauty. The sea may have become sterile, but it was stunning. The climate was temperate and the beaches were gorgeous stretches of sand. There is a sense of paradise on the northwestern coast of Sicily, exactly as there is in Monterey, Carmel, Pebble Beach, and Pacific Grove, California. It was not an accident that both areas are now considered international tourist destinations.

Northwestern Sicily could hardly be described as paradise in the early years of the twentieth century, however. Memories of poverty, which drove the migrations continuously through the 1900s, remained strong. Both Monterey Sicilians and Sicilians in Sicily spoke of past and present migrations as having a clear economic impetus. They presented, in common, that their response to the increasing scarcity of fish populations in the 1900s was a collective pattern of continuous migrations throughout the Mediterranean and North African coastal region and eventually to North America. Both populations referred to female and male migrants as though it was perfectly normal and appropriate for women to take up migration as well as men.

Women and men described the economic outlook for Sicily in the early years of the twentieth century as "hopeless." "There was no hope in Sicily," Ray Lucido explained. "You have to know the desperation of the people. Those who were fishermen saw their income depleted. It was miserable."[51] Ray and his sister Betty came to Monterey together with their mother as children in 1931. They vividly recollected the poverty of their village in Sicily, and the contrast with American life that they witnessed as children. "In Sicily we fought over a potato in the street. . . . In America you could have milk and coffee for breakfast. And meat! In San Vito we had meatballs maybe once a year. I didn't even know what a steak was. . . . Everything seemed wonderful to us in America."[52]

The narrators in this study were part of a much larger out-migration from Italy generally and Sicily in particular beginning in 1900 and lasting through the first decades of the twentieth century.[53] More a colony than a region, Sicily suffered the downside of markets and broker capitalism. Sicilians were the suppliers of labor and raw materials that made possible the industrialization and development of northern and western Europe.[54]

Widespread poverty, brought on in part by government efforts to compete with other world powers in the early decades of the twentieth century, an enforced nationalism, drought, disease (human and crop related), few opportunities for economic or social advancement, high taxes, and overpopulation were all factors that stimulated emigration from Sicily from 1880 well into the twentieth century. One quarter of the population left Italy during this time. Fully five hundred thousand Italians came to the United States in 1901 alone.[55]

The villagers of San Vito Lo Capo, Isola Della Femina, and the islanders of Marettimo recalled a fishing network that spanned the Mediterranean and took them to North Africa throughout the decades of the early twentieth century. Giovanna "Jenny" Lucido Costanza described in some detail how her mother's entire family participated in multiple migrations in order to cope with the insufficiency of resources in San Vito Lo Capo: "My mother's family moved to Tunisia to work in a fish processing plant and to fish before my mother was even born. . . . Then my grandmother got sick and the family moved back to San Vito Lo Capo. My grandmother died soon after that, and my grandfather left the children [with kin] and went to America. We had relatives in Detroit. This was 1915. He [the grandfather] worked in New York, Detroit, San Francisco, then came to Monterey. One by one he sent for the children. They came first to Detroit. My mother worked in factories there, then was able to move to San Francisco. She finally got to Monterey when she was sixteen because my grandfather had arranged for her to marry my father. She stayed here the rest of her life."[56]

Salvatore Ferrante described generations of men and women in a family on the move from Sicily to the North African coast: "I grew up with stories of my grandparents, great-grandparents, relatives, going to Africa, fishing all over the place." His own life included travels from Sicily to North Africa to America to Latin America. "I spent my childhood going back and forth from Isola Della Femina [the family village in Sicily] to Tunisia. After my father died, my uncle immigrated [to America] first. Eventually we all came. First to New York, then to San Francisco, [then] to Monterey. It was 1923. So I asked my mother and my sister and we decided to move. I worked in Monterey until 1940. Then I went to Long Beach for five years. My family, my wife, my mother, stayed here. After that, I came back here and built my own cannery. But the fish disappeared here in Monterey, so I went to Peru and built a cannery there. . . . I missed my family and I came back to Monterey for good to do consulting, a little of this or that."[57]

Once the family settled in Monterey, they never moved again. Mr. Ferrante traveled in order to find work in southern California and in the burgeoning fishing industries of Chile and Peru, but the family stayed in Monterey, and he eventually returned to Monterey to live out his remaining years.

Women and Out-Migration

What is evident in these two preceding narrative examples, and what became plain in so many others, is that the depletion of sardines and other fish populations in Sicily happened rather quickly in the early years of the 1900s, and that this created a fundamental change in the lives of many, but not all, Sicilian fisherpeople in the villages of San Vito Lo Capo and Isola Della Femina, and on the island of Marettimo. The pattern of fisherwomen staying behind to maintain homes and communities had begun to shift in these villages. Families realized that the scarcity of fish in Sicilian waters was permanent, not temporary, and the tourist industry was nowhere near the viable economic alternative in Sicily in the early decades of the twentieth century that it would become in later decades. Many Sicilians believed that new opportunities for economic survival could only be found at great distances. Many women chose to travel those distances, and so joined men in migrant streams to North Africa and North America looking for exactly the same socioeconomic advancement immigrants from elsewhere in Sicily, Italy, and the rest of southern and eastern Europe and Asia sought in these years. Like fisherpeople in other cultures, and like Sicilian women in other contexts, Monterey's Sicilian women were used to taking action, making decisions, and "taking a risk" in order to benefit themselves and their families.

Women stressed family unity as a primary motivation for making the migration a family enterprise that would be permanent rather than temporary. Vitina Spadaro is the matriarch of a large, extended family in Monterey. They began as fishers, but now own and manage several rental properties and businesses in Monterey. She explained her own migration in 1934 as prompted by an understanding on the part of so many other Sicilian fisherwomen that the typical pattern of male migration and remittances was no longer viable or desirable: "We wanted our families to be together. After many, many years of back and forth [by the men], we could see that it was better to make a living in America [rather than in Sicily]."[58] Like the immigrant women Elizabeth Ewen studied in her analysis *Immigrant Women in the Land of Dollars,* many Sicilian women migrants believed that novel forms of opportunity were going to be available to them, as well as to men, in the American setting. Ewen argued, "Money and America became synonymous and became the basis for the realization of long-standing dreams."[59] Joe Favazza reminisced about his mother's dreams and goals as a young immigrant: "When we thought about America, we thought about good things, only good things. My mother wanted to go to school. This was the country of opportunity."[60]

Mr. Favazza recalled his mother's experience as an immigrant girl in the 1920s, engaged to his father, a man she had never met: "She always said 'I couldn't wait to come to America. I left nothing there [in Sicily]. I don't wanna go back.' She thought she would get rich here. She and her sisters. They couldn't wait to come [to America]."[61] Mr. Favazza's mother worked in the canneries and bought real estate on the family's behalf. She was determined to ensure her family had a stake in the city of Monterey.

According to family histories, men usually traveled first as a measure of expediency, and in the most circuitous way, landed in Monterey. Nancy Mangiapane, whose large, extended family immigrated to Monterey by way of Chicago and Pittsburg, California, explained the common process of migration and settlement: "The best thing for them was to live all together, cheap, in a rooming house, and get some work, get the lay of the land, you know, decide if they wanted to stay, see what it was really like. Women couldn't really do that. So a man and his [grown] son or brother or father would come, and then [women in the family] would come when they could have a house. The best thing was for my father to go to New York. We had cousins there. Then after two, three months he got to Sacramento, to fish. He heard Monterey was full of sardines, so he went there. That was in the twenties. So then when he got a house we came."[62]

Transnational Identity

For Sicilian migrants, Monterey slowly emerged as a jewel of a destination site. Many families came to that realization gradually and only after trying their luck in the Midwest, in the fishing communities of Martinez and Pittsburg near Sacramento, and in San Francisco. Although some Sicilians from the coastal villages put down roots in the Midwest, particularly in Flint and Detroit, Michigan, these cities bore absolutely no resemblance to their homes in Marettimo or San Vito Lo Capo. Those who moved on explained that they did so when they heard of a chance to fish again. Both Martinez and Pittsburg, California, afforded opportunities to fish, and both of these towns developed along parallel lines to Monterey, with strong contingents of Sicilian fisherpeople linked by family and village to one another. Katherine Davi Collins wrote an exhaustive genealogical analysis of the Sicilian fishing families of Martinez, California, showing clear familial connections to Monterey families, although without the presence of Marettimares.[63] Fisherpeople in Martinez and Pittsburg fished for bass, salmon, and sturgeon. San Francisco had a booming and varied fishing industry, but one dominated by northern Italians. There, Sicilians were tightly restricted from the most profitable fishing and also reminded, clearly, of their southern Italian roots and made to feel inferior.[64]

Monterey, like Pittsburg and Martinez, seemed strikingly similar to the Sicilian coastal villages in topography, climate, and in the physical layout of the city itself, where even the poorest people could view the ocean from the windows of their homes along the wharf. Many migrants described encountering Monterey as "finding paradise." The sardines were prolific. This was the type of fishing community of which Sicilians from San Vito Lo Capo, Marettimo, and Isola Della Femina had a long history and intimate knowledge; it was their resource in the most profound way that a fishing community and a human community are connected.

Although the census is critical in documenting the actual immigration to Monterey, the oral histories provide depth and a crucial understanding of its cultural significance. Sicilians expressed awe at the striking similarities between Monterey and the villages of Sicily whence they came: "I could have been in Trapani," said Maria Mineo about Monterey upon arrival. "The whole place was familiar."[65] Again and again, migrants and their families noted the similarities of climate, coastline, flora, and fauna between Sicilian coastal villages and Monterey. It had a powerful and immediate impact. "When I came to Monterey I feel I was at home," said Mrs. Mineo, explaining that in Monterey she frequently encountered many former villagers from San Vito Lo Capo, which gave her a strong sense of belonging.[66]

In the decades following World War II, innovations in technology and transportation gave new meaning to migration and opened possibilities for both frequent contact and also more frequent returns to villages of origin. In this way, Sicilians rebuilt or maintained social and economic ties to villages that may have been interrupted during the war years but certainly contributed to a feeling on migrants' parts that they truly belonged to both the world they left and the one they currently found themselves in.

Migrants, especially third-wave migrants, expressed ambivalence about identity in their interviews: "Who am I? A little of this; a little of that. I'm an American, sure, but in my heart, I feel that [Marettimo, Sicily] is my home. We go back in the summer, most of the summers. Sometimes I feel a little strange there too," commented Anita Ferrante.[67] Her ambivalence was echoed by other narrators, who poignantly expressed the sense of transnational identity so evident in recent scholarship on immigration. Sociologist Linda Basch defined transnational communities as the "process by which immigrants forge and sustain multi-stranded social relations that link together their societies of origin and settlement . . . [immigrants] build social fields that cross geographic, cultural, and political borders . . . An essential element is the multiplicity of involvements that transmigrants sustain in both home and host societies."[68] Linda Saccomano (pseudonym), a recent immigrant and native of Trapani, considered her sense of identity: "I don't know. I guess I am a little bit of both, here and there. I live here now [in Monterey] but we go home every year for a month, two months. I feel like I am at home [in Sicily], but I feel different too."[69]

The availability of reasonably priced transportation has added an element of doubt to the whole process of migration. It is possible to decide not to decide on a permanent home site in the twenty-first century. Natale Pizzamente (pseudonym) operates a small inn with her family on the island of Marettimo during the summer months, but spends much of the winter in Monterey, working in retail shops on the wharf. It is perfectly acceptable for a single woman to travel alone at this moment in time. Ms. Pizzamente lives with cousins while she stays in Monterey in order to economize, and because it is more comfortable for her to be with family, not because she might commit a cultural faux pas by living alone.[70]

One young Sicilian mother of three in her early thirties, Ursula Anaclero (pseudonym), now makes her home in San Vito Lo Capo, a village her grandmother left in the 1920s. On one of her summer vacations to San Vito in the 1980s, Mrs. Anaclero met her Sicilian husband, fell in love, and decided to remain in Sicily. She divides her time between San Vito Lo Capo, Sicily, and Monterey, but spends the bulk of the year in San Vito Lo Capo, which she considers her primary home, although she identifies herself as an "American girl." Hers is an unusual but not unique situation. As families increasingly enjoy the luxury of travel, and descendants of migrants spend summers with extended families, there is a strong flow of migration back to original villages by newer generations.[71]

Transnational identity, in the case of Monterey's Sicilian migrants, required a sense of genuine attachment to Sicily and to Monterey. The attachment to Monterey came early on, and because women who joined migration streams made homes in Monterey. The life of Marielena Spadaro is a case in point. She is the granddaughter of women and men who migrated from the island of Marettimo, Sicily, in the 1920s. They never intended to return to Sicily. "My grandparents had bad memories of Marettimo. They wanted to make a new life here from the beginning," she explained. The family thrived in Monterey. They took advantage of the boom years of sardine fishing, in the 1920s, 1930s and 1940s. "My grandfather paid back an $80,000 loan in a year. They worked hard, saved, and really prospered here. No one ever thought of going back to live in Marettimo. But our family sent a lot of money back there, bought homes, boats for the [Marettimare relatives]."

Marielena is very clear about her own identity: "I am an Italian American. My roots are there [in Sicily], but I was brought up here, and this is my home. This is where my family is and where I want to live." However, she married a fisherman from Marettimo while he was visiting Monterey. Her husband feels less of a sense of American identity and continues to identify not just as a Sicilian but as a Marettimare. His intentions as a migrant were only to fish recreationally in Monterey, but always to return. His home was Marettimo.

With his marriage to Marielena, however, all of that changed. The couple

purchased a home next door to her parents' home in what is known as
Fisherman's Flats in Monterey. They have two children. They have visited
Marettimo several times, usually for extended periods of a month or more,
but have no intentions of living there permanently. Their children, born in
Monterey, will attend school in Monterey, and are American citizens by birth
and cultural affiliation, although they will certainly be made aware of their
Sicilian roots and will no doubt visit Marettimo many times in the course
of their childhoods. Their story encapsulates the essence of the Sicilian migration to Monterey from its inception in the 1920s to its continuation in
the present day.

Marielena's husband appeared to be the typical "sojourner" who came to
look for better economic opportunities in Monterey, but identifies strongly
as a fishermen. Marielena's family history demonstrated that the migrations
to Monterey were largely family enterprises and meant to be permanent
movements, even from the beginning of settlement. When families came to
Monterey, they came to fish, and although they moved into other businesses reflecting the new opportunities in tourism, they continued to identify as
fisherpeople and to behave economically in ways that cemented their presence in Monterey. Women in the family participated fully and actively in
both the migrant stream, in cementing an identity as fishers, and in the business enterprises that followed the economic dependence on fishing. As the
narrative illustrated, there was, and is, continuity with the past and with the
people of the homeland, the connections to which women primarily kept
alive, leading to a constant migration. Sicilians maintained a conscious attachment to the culture of Sicily and to the customs of the villages of origin,
as a matter of course, but this was intensified when it became possible to
visit the island frequently enough to make the connections real. And yet, it
was Marielena who determined the home site and the family's place of primary residence. Both Marielena and her husband feel closely attached to
Sicily, which they express through everything from menu items in their restaurants to language to their attachment to local organizations such as the
Italian Catholic Federation in Monterey. The family home is Monterey because Marielena made that choice definite, but that did not mean loss of
identity as Sicilian fishers.[72]

Catherine Caliri (pseudonym) explained how women in families made
the definitive choice of home site, even when their spouses disagreed: "We
[women] figured if the sardines could disappear from Monterey, they could
disappear from San Pedro too. We all had nice homes here. My husband
wanted to go to San Pedro. He even put a down payment on a house in San
Pedro and put our house here up for sale. But when he left we [she and her

children] took down the sign. We didn't want to leave Monterey. This was our home. When my husband realized that, he cried like a baby. It was so hard for him to sell that boat." The boat was sold, nonetheless, and the family bought small businesses and rental property in Monterey, although the male family members continue to fish on a smaller boat for recreation and to supplement the family income. Still, as with the Spadaro family, the Caliri's consciously identify as part of the community of fishing people and as active members of Monterey's Sicilian fishing community.[73]

Rose Ann Aliotti, a travel agent and member of one of Monterey's prominent fishing families, argued that the trend in migration from Sicilian villages to Monterey has continued. It is this movement that is most responsible for continued attachments: "It is common for honeymoon couples, or people who come to visit families, or to work for a few months to come to Monterey." It is the continual influx of new migrants, temporary or not, that adds ethnic vitality to a community she feels could be in danger of blending completely into the broader culture of Anglo-American Monterey.[74]

Sardines drew other ethnic fisherpeople to Monterey. Portuguese from the Azores, Yugoslavian fishermen, Mexican workers, Japanese, Chinese, and Filipinos all made critical contributions to the development of the commercial fishing industry in Monterey.[75] However, what these other ethnics did not do was to identify themselves as a Monterey ethnic fishing community. The Sicilians overcame differences based on home village to reinvent themselves as one Sicilian community of fishers largely because of the determination of Sicilian women to do so. Their choices and behavior were rooted as much in fishing culture as in being Sicilian.

The scholarly literature on Sicilian immigration recognizes women as important, even critical to the process of migration and settlement of families.[76] However, this study clearly shows that Sicilian women in Monterey, because they were also fishers, played a pivotal role in the process in reconstructing identity among disparate villagers. Also important, Sicilian women and men maintained ties to the villages that kept connections alive and allowed for the formation of the transnationalism so commonly found in the scholarly literature on Mexican, Dominican, South and Central American, and Korean immigrant groups in the late twentieth and twenty-first centuries.[77]

New Migrations, New Realities

Since the 1970s, Italy itself, and Sicily in particular, has become a destination site for many migrants from Africa and the Middle East as well as from the

Philippines, who come for the same reasons Italians emigrated in earlier decades.[78] They hope for better lives economically, socially, and politically. Frequently, immigrants to Italy engage in the same behavior as the Italian migrants to the United States once did—sending one family member to work in Italy in order to send remittances to the home country, rather than emigrating as a family group immediately.[79] However, the likeliest immigrant to contemporary Italy is female rather than male. Italian homes are cleaned by Somali and Filipino women who are supporting entire families in their homelands.[80] It has become a serious public policy issue for Italians, shared by other western European countries as well as Canada, Australia, and the United States, when these workers want to bring families and to make their migrations more permanent. "Since the 1970s . . . receiving states were trying to reassert control over migration flows . . . in response to public opinion, which was increasingly hostile to high levels of immigration."[81]

Italian visitors and immigrants post-9/11 do not express concern about the effects of restrictive legislation in the United States, as have migrants from various parts of Southeast Asia, from the Middle East and Africa, or even from other parts of Europe. Although there is a paucity of both data and new scholarship reflecting immigration realities in the post-9/11 world, Italy's relationship as a U.S. ally in the recent war with Iraq, even sending troops into the region, has ensured that the close ties of Monterey's Sicilians and their kin in Sicily have remained strong in recent months and years.

While a certain level of acculturation was taking place throughout the entire period, it was complicated by transnational identity formation brought about by constant flows of people, in both directions. Complex familial motivations inspired both emigration and immigration, particularly for women, but economics played a crucial role in the decision-making process for both sexes. The availability of work for women in Monterey fish canneries between 1920 and the 1950s affected the choices working-class Sicilian women made initially to migrate to Monterey, and then to make Monterey a permanent settlement and Sicilian fishing community.

2. Work and Identity

We were poor. Working class, I guess you would call it. God yes it was important
for us to work. I started working on the wharf at the abalone factory. We
trimmed the abalone. I was seventeen. All the women worked. We did washing,
cleaning, housework, and we also did whatever we needed to do. The men fished.
But what the husbands brought in wasn't enough, never has been. We had to
work. Somebody had to do the packing, the cleaning, the cutting, and the men
didn't do it. Women did. As soon as we heard that the fish were in, we used to get
up early. The sardines couldn't go soft; they had to be nice and firm to get into
those cans. Of course women took care of the household too; decided how much
to spend for this or that. *A woman's job was taking care of her husband and children; she took care of everything. It was a given thing. . . .*

I knew I wanted to buy a house. My dad never owned any property. We always
rented the house that we lived in. . . . I got married when I was nineteen . . . it was
up to me to figure it out. I decided to try to work something out with my land-
lady, Mrs. Sandholz . . . I called her up one day and I asked if she was willing to
sell the house. She was, and we made a deal that she would sell it to me for two
thousand dollars. I paid her a hundred dollars down and thirty dollars a month.
It took us, I guess, about ten years to pay it off. I borrowed two hundred and fifty
dollars from my older sisters for the down payment. And I paid them back eventually. We would have a good catch and my husband would bring back seven or
eight hundred dollars and I would go ahead and spread it around. But I kept a
little to keep us going. We had a charge account at a market . . . on Del Monte
Avenue and everybody went there and had a running charge account. And when
we got enough money we paid them off. Otherwise we would never have been
able to live. Everybody lived on credit.

—Interview with Lucy Ventimiglia Gruwell, September 19, 2001

The woman responsible for the preceding narrative, Mrs. Lucy Ventimiglia
Gruwell, lives in Pacific Grove. She is ninety years old but looks and acts
twenty years younger. She is tiny, full of wit and energy. She insists repeatedly that she "likes to keep [her] mind agile" and so keeps up with her son's
business, old and new friends, and hobbies. She not only recalled her early
life in Monterey vividly, but also shared keepsakes, artifacts, photographs,
and memorabilia that made her past, and that of her family and community, real for both of us.

Mrs. Gruwell's narrative is typical of poor and working class early experiences in Monterey, and illustrated several important features about the nature of the Sicilian community in Monterey in the earliest years of immigration and settlement—1915 through the 1920s. It was, first and foremost, a community economically dependent on women from the very start. The work of Sicilian women in Monterey conformed to the pattern of women's work and women's lives among fisherpeople in other communities and cultures. It was important, varied, included both reproductive and productive labor as a matter of course, and required a large measure of self-sufficiency both in the work itself and in the choices women made for the long term for their families.[1] Her narrative is a good example of how Sicilian women felt about sardine fishing generally. Sicilian women really cared whether or not the sardines would "go soft" and felt that their labor was integral to the labor of the fishermen. They did not see themselves as separate, but as a crucial part of a fishing enterprise. Moreover, their work cutting abalone and on the sardine cannery assembly line gave their families just enough in the way of extra income to become stakeholders in the city of Monterey.

Recent scholarship on Italian immigration demonstrates that the process of acculturation into the host society for Italian immigrants depended on Italians moving beyond the bounds of the Italian community. Italian immigrants made connections outside of their ethnic group largely through occupation.[2] Virginia Yans-McLaughlin's study of Buffalo, New York; Rudolph Vecoli's work on Chicago Italians; Franca Iacovetta's analysis of Italians in Toronto; and Donna Gabaccia's multiple studies of Italians in New York and in the United States generally, are all examples of how occupation shaped Italian American communities, and also pulled Italian immigrants into American (or Canadian, Australian, Latin American, etc.), culture. This was especially true for working-class immigrants, as the vast majority of Italian immigrants were working class. Participation in the formation of unions is usually cited as a particularly powerful moment, giving Italian immigrants a broader sense of cultural identity with others in the host society of their class and occupational group.[3]

In Monterey, non-Sicilian ethnic immigrant workers experienced a similar transformation and acculturation as they participated in the fishing industry. John Walton studied Monterey's numerous and diverse working-class ethnic groups and concluded that "cannery workers and fishermen . . . formed a working-class community with its own emergent culture."[4] According to Kate Davis's analysis of fish cannery workers in her study *Sardine Oil on Troubled Water: The Boom and Bust of California's Sardine Industry, 1905–1955,* 65 percent of the cannery workforce was non-Sicilian by the late 1930s, and consisted of migrant Mexican, Portuguese, Spanish, Asian, and Dust Bowl laborers. Davis meticulously documented the stages of union organization that brought this disparate mix of cannery women together to form a "cannery culture" of their own.[5]

However, fishing for Sicilian men and cannery work for Sicilian women were never just occupations in Monterey, as they were for other ethnic immigrants or for Italian or Sicilian immigrants elsewhere. Men described months on fishing boats with their relatives, brothers, fathers, and in-laws as intense, involving hard, physical labor. They also remembered barbecues and camping on uninhabited beaches after long days of fishing together. It was adventurous and dangerous and included fighting, tragic losses at sea, and cruelty among the crew. The nature of conflicts among fishermen was often related to the dynamics of working and living together on small fishing boats, whether the boats were in Sicily, Monterey, Alaska, or southern California, rather than part of the process of migration and settlement, or as a result of life in Monterey.

The narratives of women expressed a far more nuanced and compelling story about the special significance of fishing for Sicilians as a whole, and particularly wage labor in the sardine canneries for working-class Sicilian immigrant women in Monterey, which definitively separated them out from their coworkers on the cannery assembly line and made their immigration experience unique. Through their work, Monterey Sicilian women led the way to come together as a self-identified fishing community. Instead of the work assimilating the immigrants, the immigrants assimilated the work. In doing so, they invented an identity that was all their own. They remain identified as fishing people in the present day, even though very few people actually fish for a living.

Work in the Canneries

Sixty-three of the one hundred women I interviewed were age seventy or older. All but ten of those women worked in the sardine canneries at some point in their lives; some worked for years, and the majority just worked intermittently. All left as soon as it was financially possible within their family economies. No one traveled out of Monterey to work in the fruit canneries inland when the sardine season concluded every year in February. None of the women younger than sixty worked in the sardine canneries. The families had either moved into the middle class by the time younger women came of age, or if they were newer immigrants and working class, they sought

other less skilled jobs in restaurants, laundries, and retail businesses to supplement family income.

Sicilian women made up about one-third of the cannery workforce in the
1930s and 1940s. They were not the majority. However, because they formed
a solid ethnic bloc, they perceived themselves, and were perceived by coworkers, to dominate cannery work. "The Italian women really dominated. They
were really tight together, always talking Italian. They thought they were
better," remarked Mary Soto, ninety, a Portuguese immigrant cannery worker.[6] Sicilian women continuously emphasized their sense of solidarity in their
narratives, not as cannery workers but as Sicilians and fisherpeople. Lenore
Pelligrino (pseudonym), a formidable Sicilian woman even in her eighties,
was emphatic about Sicilian women's solidarity: "We all stuck up for each
other [regardless of personal differences]. We are Sicilians first."[7] The use of
language, Sicilian dialect rather than Italian, was one of the important methods Sicilian women utilized to generate a sense of solidarity and identity that
differentiated them from other workers.

Most of the non-Sicilian sardine cannery workers did not make up a permanent part of Monterey's population. They worked in the sardine fisheries
during sardine season, which lasted from August through February, then
moved to the Central Valley to work in the fruit canneries, continuously
moving to accommodate fishing and crops. Juanita Segovia, who identified
as Spanish, not Mexican, explained: "We moved regularly, from the ranches
to the fields in Hollister to the canneries [in Monterey]."[8] A few families
owned homes in several of the towns they worked in, but most owned no
property at all, barely managing to stay alive on meager incomes as migrant
laborers. Mexicans and Dust Bowl refugees in particular were ostracized in
Monterey as outsiders and undesirables by the 1930s, even though Mexican
workers had lived and worked in Monterey for two centuries.[9] The City
Directories show a huge displacement of working-class Mexicans out of
Monterey proper as new arrivals acquired property in the city.[10] When the
histories of Cannery Row were written, however, Mexicans and migrant
laborers were completely omitted from the story.[11]

Sicilian women remained clear about the limits of their identity as cannery
workers. As Mrs. Gruwell's narrative makes apparent, however, they had a
conscious appreciation of themselves as working class and as poor. Annette
Balestreri talked about the repetition, the sheer drudgery of cannery work.
She concluded, "It wasn't the best job in the world . . . but it was our bread
and butter. . . . It was what we had to do until things got better."[12]

Canning sardines required attention, stamina, and skill. Sardines were canned in the following manner by the 1920s and 1930s when Sicilian narrators worked in the canneries:

* Fish were sucked in from the floating fish hoppers, weighed, and sorted.
* By 1927 centrifugal pumps sucked sardines into the cannery at 70 tons an hour. The force and speed of this process had the bonus effect of scaling the sardines. A conveyer lifted the fish up to scales to be weighed and sorted.
* Working for 33½ cents an hour, female cannery workers placed the sardines belly-down in slots on a metal conveyor belt. The belt carried the sardines through a cutting machine that cut off their heads and tails and cut out their entrails. All the scraps were sent out to be reduced into fishmeal and oil.
* With 24 to 32 cutting machines running, [canneries] could process 1¼ tons of sardines an hour.
* Once a can was packed, it was put back onto a conveyor belt that moved it into the pre-cooker to be steamed. After steam cooking, the cans were tipped over and drained.
* Each can was squirted with sauce and then sealed by the can-sealing machine.
* Tomato, mustard, or seasoned-oil sauce was added to the steaming sardines just before the can was sealed. Conveyor belts delivered cans to this machine where they were sealed shut. Then . . . small rollers crimped the lids onto the cans. The big cylinder lifted each can into the head as its lid slid in from the stack on the right. Each pre-cooker had its own sealer and could process 45 cans a minute—2,700 an hour.
* It took two men to roll a full basket into one of the cannery's huge pressure cookers (retorts). Six to seven baskets could fit inside one retort. There, steam and pressure cooked and sterilized the fish.
* About a half an hour after opening the cannery, the packers had canned a load of fish, and the boiler operators would send steam to the retorts to cook the first batch. The boiler operator cooked batches all day long at 240 degrees for one and a half hours. . . . The sardines were cooked and sterilized inside their cans.
* Five thousand cases could be processed in a seven- or eight-hour period.[13]

Women who worked on the cannery assembly lines vividly recalled the daily stuff of their work, even sixty or seventy years later. They described the chaos at home when the cannery whistles blew at any hour of the day or night calling them to work. Women froze in the midst of cooking, cleaning, doing laundry, and tending children. Or they were jolted awake in the middle of the night. It might be two in the afternoon or two in the morning, but if the cannery whistle blew, one dropped everything and got there within forty-five minutes in order to keep one's job. Women scrambled—not knowing if they would be away from their homes and children for five hours or fifteen. "When they called, you were there," recalled Angie Bruno.[14] "I was the only one who had a car," recalled Eleanor Fugetta. "When the whistle would blow, at 2 o'clock, 12 o'clock, 11 o'clock at night, I would get up and go. I would pick up all the women in the neighborhood—Mrs. Balestreri, Mrs. Minafo, Fanny Bellar—all these women. I would pick them up and I would take them to work."[15] She was not picking up non-Sicilian women, however, and taking them to work, even though the neighborhoods were mixed; Sicilian, Japanese, Portuguese, Spanish, and Mexican people lived in close proximity to one another.[16] The camaraderie that Sicilian women described was limited to members of their own ethnic group. Through work they were forming themselves into an ethnic enclave separate from workers of different ethnicities.

"We worked HARD," was a constant refrain from women now in their eighties and nineties who remembered hours and hours of standing in line in the freezing cold, the machinery deafening, water running on the floors. The canneries in the 1930s were dank, noisy workplaces, where fourteen-year-olds worked twelve-hour shifts, six days a week, for thirty-three cents an hour.[17] "Can you imagine squeezing the guts out of fish at three or four in the morning?" said Annette Balestreri.[18] "It was like a sweathouse in the big cities," recalled Nancy Mangiapane. "They even timed us when we went to the bathroom."[19] "We used to dread getting up in the morning because we worked so hard," said Thelma Francioni.[20] "It was hell," concluded Rose Salimento.[21] One former worker remembered that some of the women got so tired they fell asleep on the job. "You had to watch them so they didn't get hurt. I was working with May Shaw and she put her head down and just fell asleep, so I did her work for her at the same time as mine," said Yvonne Russo Humbracht.[22]

Women arrived for work wearing black rubber boots, white aprons, and hair nets, which they had to provide for themselves. The warehouse was drafty, wet, cold, and steamy, with machinery running everywhere. The smell could become unendurable. "It even got into your hair."[23] Workers often felt ashamed of the smell that clung to them at the end of their shifts. Yet, at the same time, they defended themselves. They responded almost defiantly, indicating in their response that they understood their work formed a crucial basis for the development of the fishing industry as a whole, which they viewed as a benefit to the entire Sicilian community: "We would say back [to people who ridiculed the smell of sardines on women returning from work] 'You know what you smell? You smell money!' We told them."[24] Sicilian women were proud of their economic contribution to the fishing industry through work in the sardine canneries and recounted exchanges such as this, word-for-word, sixty or seventy years afterward.

Sicilian women often expressed admiration for their own youthful ability to suffer for the higher purpose of getting critical labor done. Nancy Mangiapane began working in the canneries when she was fifteen. She remembered, "It got so cold you couldn't even go to the bathroom. . . . It was noisy too—those cans sounded like motorcycles—it's amazing we can hear at all today."[25]

One of the ways Sicilian women expressed a sense of domination as well as camaraderie in the sardine cannery was through the position of floor lady or supervisor. The position of floor ladies as intermediaries between owners and workers was critical, and it was a job reserved mostly for Sicilian women because they were perceived by cannery owners as "white" in contrast to Mexican workers, for example, although some Portuguese women became floor ladies too, especially in the later years of the 1940s.[26] Floor ladies controlled everything having to do with workplace behavior that might interfere with production. Esperanza Ventimiglia Ernandes remembered limiting conversation among workers on the line. "I used to tell my girls 'just keep your hands working as fast as your mouths because if I get a bawling out [for inadequate production] then you'll get one too.'"[27] There was a certain speed that one had to work at in order to process the fish in the essential amount of time. It could be brutal. Phyllis Taormina recalled that she outpaced older workers, and generated resentment among them, requiring the floor lady to step in and move her out: "I worked fast. Real fast. One lady said 'Hey, she's leaving the guts in the fish!' I says I am not. Look at all the guts I got. You had to stick in your finger and dig out the guts. I'm not afraid to do that. And I was doing it with both hands, faster than them. She [the forelady] says 'Phyllis, I got complaints. I know you're a good worker. I'm moving you to the cans.' So she put me rolling cans. I got deaf from those cans."[28]

Rolling cans was a job considered to be a little better than cutting and packing fish. It was located upstairs in a cannery where the environment was cleaner and dryer, but much louder, so it did take a toll on one's hearing, a common complaint among women who worked there. Fewer women worked in the cans than on the assembly lines, so it was possible to talk more with less supervision. Catherine Cardinale remembered "getting" to work in the cans:

> The floor lady liked me. So she put me and my *commare* [best friend] upstairs rolling cans. She's still my best friend. I'm godmother to her son. Boy it was loud up there and you had to work really fast because you were supplying cans to all those women down there cutting fish. We were so tired. And my friend kept talking to keep herself awake. She was talking and talking. She was talking

up a storm. Finally I said, "If you don't shut up I'm going to shove one of these cans in your mouth." We laughed about it afterwards. She told my husband, "Boy you better watch out when Catherine's tired."[29]

Vicki Ruiz described the practice of "pet" or favored workers among the bosses in the fruit and vegetable canneries. In those canneries the supervisors were usually Italian and the workers Mexican or Russian Jewish immigrants. The practice of making "pets" out of workers also took place in the fish canneries. Floor ladies used their power to place friends and relatives in work areas that were somewhat better or better placed than others. That usually meant that Sicilians generally had opportunities for advantage because so many floor ladies could be kin or friend. They could show favoritism by ignoring (or paying attention to) frequent visits to the bathroom, conversation among workers, or slower work. They could ignore seniority and give friends or relatives priority in terms of placement. Lucy Ventimiglia Gruwell commented that "power went to their [the floor ladies'] heads a little bit."[30]

Unions

Sicilian women demonstrated their sense of separate identity most clearly in their reluctance to participate in unions, in stark contrast to cannery workers of other ethnicities. Sicilians were busy coming together into a distinctive community bound by fishing and work in the fish canneries. They were not assimilating themselves into a broader culture of American workers. Conditions in the canneries were often unfair and exploitative, but Sicilian women accepted that as a normal part of life as a working person. "What are you going to do?" shrugged Angie Bruno. "If you wanted a job, that's what you had to do."[31] Yet while Sicilian men organized early on, demanding a share of the profits from fishing, Sicilian women were reluctant to do so. Lucy Ventimiglia Gruwell commented, "We just didn't see much point in a union. I joined, sure, in 1937, but I was too busy with the children, the housework, and cannery work to bother with all that. We left it to the men. We saw our work as extra."[32]

On the other hand, she emphasized the role her own father played in creating a union for working-class fishermen in Monterey:

My father started the first fisherman union here in 1927. His name was Orazio Ventimiglia. The boat owners weren't giving the fishermen a good deal. The fishermen weren't getting enough money. So my dad organized the union so the fishermen would get a fair share of what they caught. He thought of the idea of shares of everything the fishermen caught, instead of the old way of just letting the boat owners decide how much to give the fishermen. The union he started was with the AF of L. It was located in San Francisco, and my father knew the people who were involved with the fishermen's union there. He had the fishermen give so much money every time they got a paycheck. He would have insurance for the fishermen through that fishermen's union. He would put all the money in a big trunk that he had in the bedroom. He would dole it out as it was needed. My mother stayed out of the union organizing. Of course she worked at the canneries for a while. But she got sick and died young. She was fifty-two at the time.[33]

Sicilian men supported the American Federation of Labor (AFL) over the more radical Congress of Industrial Organizations (CIO). Some Sicilian men came together to buy canneries themselves. Although this often created a conflict of economic interest and hard feelings within the community of Monterey Sicilians, it nonetheless did not inhibit the formation of that community as an ethnic enclave of fishers. Sicilians may have distinguished themselves along class lines from the beginning of settlement, as I explain in the next chapter, but they continued to find ways of identifying as a Sicilian fishing community in spite of internal conflicts and disparities of wealth.

Male organizers, for their part, eventually came to appreciate the potential of female fish cannery workers as members of the union, in spite of the disinterestedness of Sicilian women in the process. "The [fish] cannery workers made up the largest union on the [Monterey] Peninsula," recalled John "Bricky" Crivello, the business agent for the Fishermen's Union of America in Monterey. "There were two, three thousand of them."[34]

Monterey fish cannery workers remained unorganized in the 1930s, however. Some of that was because of the enormous conflict that their husband fishermen were undergoing between association with the AFL and the CIO. Correspondence between officers in the American Federation of Labor, 1937–1939, showed that cannery workers had been overlooked by the AFL until the CIO organizers threatened to undermine the AFL efforts toward fishermen by organizing cannery workers. AFL union organizers grew increasingly aware that cannery workers could play a significant role in the local labor movement. "The United Fishermen of the Pacific CIO affiliate filed their petition with the NLRB. . . . They are asking for an election of the Cannery Workers Union, which has been established since 1937 meant also to get at us, the Seine and Line Fishermen's Union of Monterey, because the Cannery Workers and Fishermen are all in one industry and one can not do without the other. The United Fishermen of the Pacific knew they had no chance with the fishermen so they asked for an election of the Cannery

Workers, in other words they did not ask for an election with the Fishermen directly but indirectly thru the Cannery Workers."[35]

A local representative of the AFL wrote to the AFL legal counsel for help in alerting the union bosses about the critical need to organize the cannery workers: "I am trying to get an agreement between the cannery workers and ourselves in the event that the CIO will come here and make trouble again this coming season which I am sure they will." This representative went on to complain about the "poor support we got" from the AFL in San Francisco and how "disgusted" the Monterey fishermen felt about it. He urged, "You must get Mr. Ventimiglia [Mrs. Gruwell's father] to get busy on the NLRB to certify these cannery workers here, and you must get Mr. Lucido to understand how important it is to get the Fish Cannery Workers to come into the [union] because it proved to be a failure to fight alone even though we are all members of the AFL. The fishermen and cannery workers must be together and have a solid front to fight the CIO." The majority of non-Sicilian fish cannery workers supported the CIO but were deliberately excluded when it was time to vote for a union. The AFL simply scheduled a vote after the sardine season had ended and migrant fish cannery laborers were already gone; they were at work in the fruit canneries inland.[36]

The leadership of the AFL evidently got the message that cannery workers were critical to the union. The sheer number of cannery workers gave the industry as a whole a power it would not have had otherwise. One letter from the AFL's western director acknowledged the significance of female cannery workers to union organization: "The American Federation of Labor has given serious consideration to the welfare of the workers in the fishing and fish cannery industries . . . we have found that the most important and most valuable asset the workers in these industries could have would be a single, autonomous unit where leadership could be developed and established along the entire Pacific Coast in a powerful fishing and fish cannery organization."[37]

For Sicilians at least, fishing in Monterey wove ethnicity, class, occupation, and gender together in such a way that no one aspect of a person's life could be considered separately. The definition of being Sicilian fisherpeople may not have allowed for radical labor activism, which required a more particular sense of identity based mainly on occupation and class. The most striking aspect of Sicilian cannery workers' lives was their lack of self-perception as industrial workers, in sharp contrast to Italian cannery workers in the fruit industry and elsewhere, and also Portuguese, Mexican, and sardine cannery workers who had migrated from the Dust Bowl.[38] They seemed to go along with the formation of the unions primarily because their families supported the AFL. Angie Bruno remembered her days as a cannery worker with some sense of disdain for Sicilian women's general disinterestedness in unionization: "We were like sheep. They said to join the union, so we did."[39] Sicilian women expressed a perception of identity as working class as too limited, and never seemed to believe that unions alone would allow them the upward economic mobility they sought. Eleanor Fugetta, like so many other Sicilian women, was suspicious of the power of unions to change their lives in any significant way: "[The union] was okay. It didn't really get me anywhere. You just do what you're doing; you're not going to get any higher—union or no union."[40]

The organization of cannery workers into the AFL benefited cannery workers, however, and it was clear from the interviews that this was something former workers understood and appreciated. The favoritism of floor ladies was minimized by union rules and presence. The union also ensured higher pay, overtime pay, and a measure of job security and seniority rights. Sicilian women seemed satisfied with these gains, and did not push for more radical changes to the structure of the industrialized cannery. Nancy Mangiapane recalled, "I don't know when the union started, but when it [the union] came our wages started going up a little at a time, and then we got time and a half and double time and even a little health insurance. I went on strike a couple of times, I think. It was good that we were getting a good price for our work. I started at twenty-three cents an hour [at age thirteen], and sometimes we didn't even have a ten-minute break. We would work sixteen hours straight. Sometimes we hardly got to come home for Christmas dinner."[41]

Portuguese, Mexican, Spanish, and Anglo women felt differently. Joann Silva (pseudonym), who was Portuguese and had emigrated with her family from Hawaii in 1924, said, "We [Portuguese workers] supported the CIO. They were for the poor people."[42] Dorothy Wheeler, a Dust Bowl migrant, explained the consensus among non-Sicilian cannery workers: "A group of us could see that we weren't getting ahead. We wanted to better ourselves. It was a powerful feeling, but we were scared too. We went to a lot of meetings, and the men led, of course. But there were a few women who spoke their piece."[43] One Sicilian cannery worker, Thelma Francioni, who worked in the canneries through the 1920s, recalled, "The Spanish girls organized the unions."[44] Carmen Mercedes, a Mexican American union spokeswoman, went to different canneries to recruit. "It was exciting . . . the meetings, the strikes," recalled several former workers.[45] In fact, they eagerly anticipated the union: "They were talking for a whole year before we got it in '37. And we were all hoping because we knew we'd get more money," said Dorothy Wheeler.[46]

When the AFL finally included women fish cannery workers into its ranks, little attention was given to gender issues. Child care remained a women's issue, rather than a family issue, and continued to be a major logistical problem for most cannery workers and was only slightly overcome with innovations in technology that led to more regular and predictable work schedules. However, Sicilians in Monterey were re-creating a community of fishers in which traditional gender roles with regard to labor did not apply. Fishermen often took on more domestic roles when they were at home for stretches at a time, while fisherwomen accepted traditional male responsibilities when they were left alone for extended periods. In Monterey, fishing alternated with canning so that men could occasionally be home to watch their children while women worked in the canneries. "My husband watched the kids. He even hung out the laundry. He knew how it was for me, working in the canneries," said Rose Salimento. "Sure, I helped her," said her husband George. "She was working, working. I would keep an eye on the kids, give them a bath, clean up the house a little." He remembered doing the laundry: "I would hang up the clothes, clean the [kitchen] floor. She [his wife] was tired [after work]. Sometimes I would put on a pot of soup or something."[47]

More often, fishermen left for extended periods of time and Sicilian women utilized female support systems within kin and community. Non-Sicilian women had to figure out day care however they could. It did not occur to anyone to create day care on the job. Unionized cannery workers in Fullerton, however, fought for on-site day care in the 1940s and won it.[48] Cannery owners became so desperate for laborers during the period of World War II that they set up a day-care center to encourage mothers to come to work in the canneries.[49] Few Sicilian women took advantage of that opportunity, however, preferring either kin networks for child care or abandoning cannery work if they were economically able to do so when they were pregnant or at home with very young children. Catherine Cardinale described a fairly common pattern of work for Sicilian women, who were intimately connected with all aspects of fishing, not simply the wage labor of work in the canneries:

> I was seventeen years old and a newlywed when I did cannery work. I used the money for extras for my household. Some of the girls I worked with were my age, but most of them were older, women who could be my aunts or grandmothers. These women helped me, supported me. They knew what they were doing—they worked in the canneries all of their adult lives. They were the ones who saw changes as conditions and wages improved with the introduction of unions and new technologies. . . . I didn't work in the canneries for very long. I quit after a couple of years—after I started having children. It was important

work for me because I always knew I could go back to it if I needed to or just wanted to. For example, my husband was a fisherman who spent weeks away from home. When he was gone, I could work in the canneries. When he was home, I could stay home. One time, the floor lady called me to ask me to come in, but I refused because my husband was home. I'll never forget it. She hollered (to him really) "Joe, it's *your* fish we have to pack here!" They didn't like it when I wouldn't come in, but it didn't mean much—it wasn't like I couldn't go back when I wanted to.[50]

Catherine Cardinale did not send her small children to union day-care centers in order to work in the cannery. Eleanor Fugetta described a typical pattern of shared child care that Sicilian women utilized because they had settled in Monterey and had established fairly widespread family networks early on, unlike their counterparts who migrated for cannery work: "My sister Dolly had five kids, and she didn't work as steady [as I did], so she always took care of mine too. I worked [pregnant] until I started showing. Then I quit. I went back to work when my babies were a month old. But we worked seasonal, so that helped."[51]

When Catherine Cardinale was a child she was sent to live with her grandparents during the week when her mother worked in the canneries. She would come home on weekends to be with her mother and ailing father, who could no longer work as a fisherman because of a heart condition. "It was great," remembered Catherine. "My grandparents were very strict with their own children, but they spoiled me. My aunt, who was only a few years older than I, was my designated baby-sitter and was forced to take me everywhere she went, which she just hated. My Nonna [grandmother] wouldn't let my aunt have a cookie before dinner, for instance, but I always got what I wanted." Mrs. Cardinale's grandparents lived just around the corner from her parents, so it was easy to be in close touch with her mother and father, to stop by for lunch often.[52] In this way, bonds within the tight circle of Sicilian families were reinforced by women's work in the canneries.

Unions ensured on-the-job nurses for cannery workers. But the nurses were not professionals. The Sicilians who owned canneries hired nurses from the ranks of workers related to cannery owners, who acquired a minimal amount of training in order to perform the most rudimentary first aid. Phyllis Taormina worked as a nurse in her cousin's cannery. She had left school at eighth grade. "I had to go to school again for a little bit. It wasn't much. But they had to have a nurse. I went to Salinas to get my papers so I could be a nurse. You had to learn about cuts and everything. How to take care of people."[53] Workers related to owners made it difficult to separate interests along class lines. It was clear that a community was forming based at once on ethnicity and fishing, and that women played critical roles in making links along ethnic and occupational lines apparent.

Unions fought for disability and unemployment benefits for fishermen, but did not acknowledge the special problems women in their prime child-bearing years were faced with. The unions ensured only that women who were pregnant were not automatically fired; they allowed for leaves of absence for women immediately after childbirth without loss of pay. Working conditions that were acceptable for women under normal circumstances became unduly harsh during pregnancy. "Work was a lot harder when you were pregnant," said Esperanza Ventimiglia Ernandes in something of an understatement.[54] Women stood for hours. "Your legs would get so tired they ached. . . . Boy, if they let you have a little rest on a stool you were glad of that," remembered Mrs. Ernandes, who, like many other workers, wore a corset to hide her pregnancy until she was in her fifth month.[55] Two floor ladies estimated that they walked twenty or thirty miles a day, even during pregnancy. They remained philosophical about it: "If you feel well pregnant, you'll feel better working than sitting at home." Yet the cost could be high, and they were aware of the health risks of hard physical labor during pregnancy. "It took a lot out of me," said Yvonne Russo Humbracht.[56] Many suffered miscarriages and lifelong back and leg problems as a result, and anyone who could do so quit work as soon as possible into a pregnancy. Non-Sicilian women did not have that option, however. Canneries may have been more responsive to the physical needs of women workers if unions had a labor force that was less flexible, more radical, and less willing to accept poor working conditions. Sicilian women constituted a formidable block against any effort on the part of workers to make demands on canneries that might have benefited their non-Sicilian coworkers who did not have access to the community supports that Sicilians had.

Sicilian women believed in the possibility of upward mobility in Monterey's newly industrialized fisheries. Sicilian fisherwomen generally had little formal education. They were not politically naive, however, and were acutely aware of the injustices they suffered as workers. Yet, as Donna Gabaccia argued, Italian immigrant workers generally did not ask or expect much from union activity, and they did not look to radical politics or the state for help in alleviating their difficulties.[57] There was such a sense of freedom from the doomed economy of Sicily and hope for the future in the bountiful Monterey Bay that Sicilians felt little need for radical labor activism.

Exploitation by family members who were owners of canneries generally was often rationalized by narrators as necessary. Workers believed they were just "helping" family members, not being abused or exploited themselves.

For example, Phyllis Taormina worked in her cousin's cannery in various odd jobs. She worked as a nurse and also regularly made cakes and coffee to sell to workers, but lost money in the process because she paid for all supplies, including first-aid items, out of her own pocket. "I did it to help my cousin," she explained. "He was just starting out. . . . Families were very, very poor. Women, children, everyone was expected to work hard for the family, and the only place to work then was in the canneries."[58]

Esperanza Ventimiglia Ernandes began work at the canneries at age fourteen, first cutting abalone, then as a worker at Booth's cannery. "It didn't bother me to quit school to work in the canneries. It just came naturally to work. I wanted to help my family. I gave all my money to my mother," she said. "I used to work with my sister, Mamie, who was only a year younger. We used to stick together with all the other Italian girls."[59] Mrs. Ernandes was quickly promoted to floor lady, where she remained for the next six years.

She met her husband at the age of eighteen, while she worked as floor lady for Booth's Cannery. "Booth's Cannery was out on Fisherman's Wharf, separated from the Row, so it was okay for the Italian girls to work there. The Row was known to be kind of a bad place and the men didn't want the girls working out there at first. When Booth's closed, I couldn't continue working because I would have had to work on the Row. But then, a lot of Italian girls went to work on the Row after Booth's closed, and it turned out okay. It wasn't such a bad place after all."[60]

Sicilian women expressed ambivalence, even resistance, on the part of Sicilian parents about cannery work for young, single girls. The critical issue was not the work itself but the fact that the canneries in the 1920s and 1930s happened to be located in what was then the red light district of Monterey. Sicilian fisherpeople, like fisherpeople everywhere, needed and expected women to be full participants in the many important forms of labor that fishing always involved. However, for women to work among prostitutes and next to bars was a different matter. Sicilian workers were sensitive about perceptions of their respectability, and yet Sicilian women defied convention when they believed their workforce participation mattered to their families. "Cannery Row was a little rough. There were some people who, you know, slept around. People were afraid to send their [wives, daughters, sisters] down there."[61] Geno Marazzini (pseudonym), a former fisherman, defined "good girls" as ones who stayed home. "We did not want them to work anyplace, to go around with strangers."[62] Arturo Pagnini (pseudonym), whose family emigrated from Marettimo in the mid 1930s, claimed that "None of the women in my family worked. We didn't think it was right for them."[63]

Women nonetheless insisted that their work was both necessary and respectable. "They [new arrivals from Sicily] called us *puttanes* [whores]," recalled Nancy Mangiapane, who worked in the fish canneries in Monterey with her mother and aunts beginning in the 1930s: "My mother got so mad. She went right up to those men and shouted at them, 'We are decent. We are working to support our children, our families.' Boy, she told them."[64] Mary Buffo, a gentle, soft-spoken, eighty-five-year-old, related how she explained to a friend of her brother's who had recently arrived from Sicily: "Listen. I come to work to feed my family."[65]

Rose Cutino recalled her efforts to join the world of cannery workers in spite of the objections of her husband, who felt the wharf area was too rough an environment in the 1930s: "I was barefoot! Barefoot! We were so poor I didn't have shoes! And still he [her husband] said, 'No you're not going to work.' I cried. I begged him. But he wouldn't let me. I had to get out of the house. Just for a little while, you know. I wanted to be with my *cammares* [girlfriends]. They were all working. And I didn't have shoes. I was ashamed." This woman recalled her exasperation at trying to convince her husband that she needed to work for the good of the family. Desperation finally required drastic measures. "I got a very bad headache. I went to bed for a few days. He finally said, 'Okay. You can go to work.' I was so happy."[66]

Women consciously challenged what they perceived to be unfounded objections to their workforce participation. After all, productive labor was always something fisherpeople accepted for both sexes. "It was what we had to do, we worked for the family. It was a family decision."[67]

Significant improvements in working conditions came with new technology in the 1940s and led to a general acceptance on the part of Sicilians that Cannery Row was less threatening, simply a place to work. Instead of bars, canneries dominated the wharf area by the 1940s. New methods of processing fish, specifically refrigeration, meant that women did not have to rush to the canneries as soon as the sardines were brought in, working until all the fish were processed. "It was still hard work, factory work. It was wet and cold and you could always smell the fish. Still, we didn't have to wait for cannery whistles. We got a phone call. We didn't have to go in to work at all odd hours, we could work from 8 A.M. to 5 P.M. and plan for our child care and our schedules. Technology had improved and fish could be kept until we came to can them. They did not need to be canned just as they were unloaded off the boat. When there was a big catch and we worked overtime, we got paid for overtime—that was an important difference between my experience and the experience of women in the earlier generation who worked before unions were put in place, and conditions were a little rougher and more primitive."[68]

Sicilian women identified wholly with all that they did, not just what they did for wages. Angie Bruno phrased it most succinctly: "I'm an Italian. I'm a homemaker. I'm a cannery worker. No stopping. It was all one day. I did everything. I was all of it."[69] Dolly Ursino contemplated the meaning of work in the sardine canneries, where she worked seasonally from the age of seventeen until her marriage at age twenty-one: "We were cannery workers, sure.... But the most important thing was being Italian, being part of our families."[70]

Mexican women's work in the fruit canneries utilized kin and family to strengthen both ethnic and occupational identity, and also to gain a foothold in American society. However, they stopped short of creating an identity as agriculturalists out of their experience, as the Sicilians did as fisherpeople. According to Ruiz and Zavella, Mexican fruit cannery laborers came together as workers. They did not blend ethnicity and farming in the same way that Monterey's Sicilian women fused ethnicity with fishing to construct something new, separate, and lasting. The goal of Mexican cannery workers, as well as Italian workers in the fruit industry, was to blend into the middle-class American mainstream, not to create a discrete ethnic entity.

Beyond the Cannery

The definition and conceptualization of "work" incorporated cannery work, housework, child care, taking in boarders, finances that sometimes included money lending, and a particular kind of kin-work for Sicilian women without clear distinctions made. When asked about the work they did, Sicilian cannery workers were as likely to discuss housework, embroidery or rosary groups, child care, or organizing events with the Italian Catholic Federation as they were to discuss experiences on the factory floor: "We used to cook, clean, do our laundry, bake our bread. The children were always clean and well fed. Our homes were spotless.... We embroidered, crocheted, made trousseaus for our daughters [and] our nieces, cooked and cleaned for all of our relatives."[71]

The essential face presented to the family, to the community, and to the world at large was a quiet, smiling nonchalance, a shrugging good-natured acceptance of the great burdens of family, household, and often cannery work as well. "It sure was hard, working all day in the canneries, then taking care of the house, the children. But when you're young you can do anything. Even when you don't feel like it you can get up and do your work," said Rose Salimento.[72]

Anna Grillo (pseudonym) described how women participated in money lending in the earliest years when acquiring credit was particularly difficult for immigrant Sicilians: "You know, let me tell you . . . Nancy's grandmother was married three times. She was a Teresi. Widowed? No, No—Divorce! And in those days it was pretty amazing for a woman to do that. But she really got the money thing. She used to charge interest! 'Honey,' she would say, 'I'll loan you a hundred dollars but you gotta pay me back a hundred and ten.' And she bought a house and made it. She never went to school either."[73]

A woman was also held accountable for, and controlled, the critical work of kinship. For Sicilian women this work of kinship meant endless but requisite visiting of in-laws and relations, and extending the proper hospitality to them in return, as a show of respect. This process of visiting never extended beyond the boundaries of other Sicilian families, however, even though many other ethnic groups participated in fishing and lived in the same neighborhoods as Sicilians. "Oh how we cooked!" remembered Rose Cutino. "I didn't just make one pie—I made three. I constantly made cookies, spaghetti, everything. I had a table that went from the kitchen to the living room. Everyone who came to my house had a place at the table. My parents came for dinner every night. My two brothers-in-law would come with their families. It was always like a *festa*. I worked so hard. . . . Saturdays were big washing and ironing days . . . we were always busy."[74]

Sicilian women attended (and brought appropriate gifts to) countless baptisms, showers, weddings, funerals, first communions, and confirmations. Added to the tasks of keeping up home and hearth, the workload was enormous. It was also evidence of the complexity of work that created a community out of an economic immigration. With women involved, work had many layers and multiple meanings, but it did not involve anyone who was non-Sicilian. Sicilian women in their mid-sixties described their mothers' kin work in action: "How she worked, [our] mother. She worked so hard. She did everything—the baking, the cooking, the laundry, the cleaning, always pregnant, always with a baby in her arms." Moreover, anyone who dropped in to visit was expected to have a meal with the family. Mothers provided it. Daughters helped.[75]

Failure to attend an event such as a baby shower or a funeral wake, or failure to bring the proper present, conveyed a hostile message. This could result in a grudge between whole families that might carry on for decades. "When a woman didn't like this person or that one, and her husband might ask her to send that person some fish, she would send over the head and tail rather than the choice center piece. That would get the point across real quick. Sometimes people didn't speak after that."[76] Excluding an obviously close relation from a wedding or even a bridal or baby shower was also an effective way to ignite or extend a bitter feud that could last for years. However, like the disputes between Sicilian fishermen and Sicilian cannery owners, these conflicts were hardly fatal to the formation of a fishing community, as I show in the next chapter. Some families might not speak to others, but they still attended the same Sicilian fishing events and continued to identify as community members.

Ownership

Wage labor in the form of work in the fish canneries of Monterey was exactly the advantage Sicilian fisherwomen needed to direct the course of migration for their families, and ultimately, for their community as a whole. Fisherpeople always expected women to engage in productive labor, and wage labor gave Sicilian fisherwomen a modicum of financial power, which they exercised to the fullest. Sicilian women remained tightly integrated into their ethnic community and even reshaped it to construct their own version of what it meant to be fisherpeople in Monterey. Most important, they used their traditional independence as fisherpeople and their newfound independence and financial power to claim a stake both in the city of Monterey and in the economy of fishing.

Working-class Sicilian women who labored on cannery assembly lines never saw their jobs as something they would always have to do. There was evidence all around them of opportunity, if not for themselves, then for their children. "My children never worked in the canneries. . . . They got good educations . . . they have good jobs. . . . I gave my children whatever they needed to do better."[77] Rose Marie Cutino Topper summarized the prevailing sentiment for women who came of age in the 1950s and 1960s, whose mothers immigrated to Monterey and worked in the canneries in the 1920s and 1930s: "Our mothers wanted us to finish high school. Then the big thing was to get a job in a bank. That was something."[78] The ascendancy of Sicilian cannery workers from working class to middle class in Monterey parallels that of Italians in Micaela di Leonardo's study of Oakland, and Glenna Matthews's analysis of Italians in San Jose.[79] Patricia Zavella and Vicki Ruiz show, in their respective studies of Mexican immigrant workers, that Mexican ethnics also used strategies such as home ownership and education to move their children from working to middle class.[80]

However, in contrast to fruit and vegetable cannery workers in other parts of California, and in contrast to Italian immigrants generally, Sicilian women in Monterey clung to an identity as fishers, whether they attained middle-class status or not. When di Leonardo's Italian immigrants achieved middle-class status and when Matthews's San Jose Sicilians did so, they abandoned their identity as cannery workers or even as agriculturalists. They were eager to lose that part of their ethnic identity that might have tied them too closely to the image of working-class immigrant and thereby inhibit acceptance into the American middle-class mainstream. Monterey's Sicilian women, on the other hand, worked even harder to retain their identity as fisherpeople, which incorporated fishing as an identity with ethnicity and with the environment of Monterey itself.

According to tax assessors' records, female initiative toward the goal of property ownership was the norm for Sicilian women in Monterey. This was the norm for ethnic women elsewhere as well. Patricia Zavella documented how Mexican women focused the family economy on home ownership, as did Glenna Matthews in her study of women of Italian, Mexican, and Korean descent in Silicon Valley. Micaela di Leonardo demonstrated the crucial role home ownership played for Italian immigrant families in California in allowing them entrance into middle-class life.[81]

The most important aspect of cannery work for Sicilian women in Monterey was that it allowed them just enough economic leverage within their families to achieve the goal of purchasing a stake in the city of Monterey, beginning with home ownership, and often expanding into rental property and small businesses. Sicilian women in Monterey already had the power of the purse within their families, in part because they came from fishing cultures and in part because Sicilian women generally controlled family finances. Cannery work increased that power just enough to move a family from working to middle class. It could not have supported a working-class family year-round, but in the case of the Sicilians, it was not meant to. Kate Davis argued that sardine cannery work was "the highest paid factory labor," which gave Sicilian families an infusion of cash that Sicilian women made the most of.[82]

What was unusual about Monterey's Sicilian fisherwomen was that they went beyond the usual investment in family homes and bought rental and commercial property as well. Pat Spadaro recalled a time when her mother, a newly arrived migrant who was unable to speak English, bought a piece of property while Pat's father was at sea, fishing. "My father just laughed about it when he came home and found out. He thought it was fine for her to do that."[83] Joe Favazza remembered a larger investment on his mother's part: "My mother . . . bought a whole city block in Monterey. She was a strong woman. She was a powerhouse. Busy, busy, busy. She worked in the canneries. She put every penny we had into buying real estate here."[84] Mary Bispo, Lena Bolle, Vita Bruno, Domenica Enea, and Anna Mello are Sicilian women who owned property in their own names as early as 1924 in Monterey.[85] The 1926 Monterey city directory reflected a population of working-class fishers with a sprinkling of Sicilian-owned groceries and bars. By 1951, out of a population of nineteen thousand, fully one-third of Monterey's homes and small businesses were owned by Sicilians.[86] Moreover, the tax assessors' records showed a dramatic increase in property ownership on the part of well-known Sicilian fishing families between 1920 and 1961.[87] Several Sicilian families added three to five new properties to their family estates every year after 1920.[88] More than half of these were owned jointly by male-female couples, presumably husbands and wives for the most part. From 10 to 20 percent were owned solely by women beginning in 1924. The rest were owned by men alone. The high percentage of female-only and female-male property owners was striking, and showed the active interest on the part of Sicilian migrant women in owning real estate, even in their own names.[89]

The Sicilian community that women helped create survived numerous economic stresses, such as the loss of the sardines in the 1950s. "Women knew it was going to end [the abundance of sardines]; they knew their future was not in fishing. Women controlled everything. They knew they were responsible. They handled all of the money, all of the investments. As soon as you had a little money, you bought another house. The women in the families invested in real estate, in small businesses. That's why [Sicilians] prospered here."[90] This was a common sentiment, especially among families who achieved middle- and upper-middle-class status through investments in real estate. Women were given much if not all of the credit for managing money wisely and investing mostly in real estate, rather than in fleets of fishing boats. They supported the fishing industry with investment, to be sure, but they did so with an eye to long-term settlement in Monterey. None of the 150 narrators I interviewed admitted absolute failure in the aftermath of sardine fishing, suggesting that financial failure was something shameful, not something one would want to admit, and also that those Sicilian women who failed at finances may have become invisible in Monterey's Sicilian fishing community.

Women from boat-owning families participated in the expansion of the fishing industry by supporting family purchases of purse seines, larger and more efficient boats that could bring in significantly bigger catches of sardines.[91] Peter Cutino, whose family was one of the original fisher families in Monterey and whose father owned a purse seine, explained that these were expensive boats and argued that the consent of women in households was requisite before such an enormous purchase could be made, or debt added, to the family economy.[92] Mike Maiorana, also from a long-standing and

successful Monterey Sicilian fisher family, maintained that it was common
for homes to be mortgaged in order to buy boats, something that must have
proven disastrous to some families when the sardine era ended. Middle-class
Sicilian fisherwomen not only had to be consulted, but also had to support
any efforts on the part of men in families to increase investment in fishing,
indicating a power of the purse that set them apart from other middle-class
Italians in California.[93] "Women had to go along [with the purchase of bigger boats] or they [their fathers] couldn't have done it. You couldn't take
that kind of money out of the family without the mother."[94] Catherine Cardinale credited her mother's support for her own family's ability to buy a
purse seine: "My mother gave [us] the money for [our] boat." Mrs. Cardinale's mother had been a floor lady in the canneries and her father owned
a small business in Monterey. After his premature death, her mother ran the
business and also helped her son-in-law gain a foothold in the burgeoning
sardine industry by becoming a boat owner early on. "My husband was the
youngest boat owner. They called him 'The Baby,'" Mrs. Cardinale recalled.[95]

Sicilian female fisherpeople, with their long history of self-sufficiency, did
not hesitate to work for wages and to act decisively to meet their goals of
economic stability and independence in order to purchase a stake in Monterey. Their laboring lives were complex, communal, and multifaceted. The
working class used the cannery as a means of access to public space and
cannery work as a way of acquiring the extra income that would allow them
to accumulate the property that would bring them into the ranks of the
middle class. The middle class invested in the larger boats and canneries that
made the industry prosper. Almost everyone bought real estate. They made
a lasting community in Monterey based on their self-identities as fully par-
ticipating members of the world of fishing. Sicilian women were not peripheral but essential to the enterprise of fishing in Monterey, and more important, in assimilating fishing itself to create an identity based on a fusion of
ethnicity, environment, and occupation. This did not mean that there were
no differences among Sicilians. Community did not mean sameness or absolute conformity and love. The difference between owning a boat and just
working on one was the first economic marker among Sicilians in Monterey,
but there were many others. As Sicilians engaged in the process of settlement
in Monterey, they created tension too.

3. Family, Conflict, Community

What is family here? I will tell you what it became. It became this interlocking
network of fishermen. There was this intensive activity, intermarriage, so that the
community is truly linked by blood. Family was the entire group. We were put
together by age groups. Children were raised together as cousins. We had the
same values, traditions—we even had the same thing for dinner every night—
right down to material possessions. Everyone had the same thing. Everyone is
related to everyone.
—Interview with Peter Cutino, August 12, 2004

In Monterey it was family to family. That's how we got along.
—Interview with Vita Crivello Davi, October 2, 1998

The preceding narratives from Peter Cutino and Vita Crivello Davi expressed
the passion and power of Sicilian family and community life in Monterey.
It was echoed by narrators who also described extremely close connections
between individuals and couples that began in their childhoods. It was clear
from the narratives that while women and men acted together to accomplish
their goal of community building, Sicilian women actually did much more
to shape their families into a clearly defined ethnic fishing community. They
arranged social get-togethers, influenced choices of marriage partners, and
even followed the same pattern of family dinner menus. They needed to do
so. Records of marriage licenses issued in Monterey between 1906 and 1979
suggested that high rates of intermarriage with outsiders early on may have
stimulated Sicilians to be purposeful, to create as closed a community among
themselves as they could in order to resist complete assimilation into mainstream American culture. It was clear from their efforts that the preservation
of Sicilian values and culture was of critical import to them.

The records showed that the highest levels of intermarriage with non-
Sicilians, mostly Spanish/Mexicans, occurred in the 1906–23 and 1923–26
recording periods. In fact, in the period 1923–26, twenty-nine out of the
fifty Sicilians sampled who acquired marriage licenses married non-Sicilians.
Eleven of the twenty-nine marriages were with people with Spanish/Mexican

surnames, and ten of the twenty-nine were cases of Sicilian girls marrying non-Sicilians. One would expect the opposite: the lowest rates of intermarriage in the earliest years of immigration, and the highest rates of intermarriage only over time, and after generations of settlement. One might also expect to see very low rates of intermarriage, if any, between Sicilian girls and non-Sicilian boys.[1]

This random sampling of marriage licenses suggests an assimilation process by way of marriage into the larger Monterey community that coincided with first migrations and early settlement. It was abruptly reversed after 1926. The period 1926–42 showed a marked decline in marriages outside the Sicilian community, with only twelve of the fifty marriage licenses issued with non-Sicilians. That pattern persisted until 1967, when once again, marriages with outsiders surpassed marriages with other Sicilians. The years between 1926 and 1967 marked the time when community building was at its peak, and the least intermarriage occurred.[2]

The fact that Sicilians did not arrive in Monterey as one group or at one moment in time, but came from rival fishing villages in Sicily, was their first challenge. They needed to move beyond boundaries based on village loyalty to come into a new perception of who they were as Monterey Sicilian fishers. The second major challenge to community building involved class differences. Sicilians faced marked economic distinctions from the moment they arrived, and they needed to find creative ways to come together as a community of equals, although some families had so much more in the way of property and material goods than others, in contrast to Mr. Cutino's assertion in the opening narrative. Sicilians needed to overcome all sorts of differences among themselves in order to create some semblance of a real, rather than assumed, community of Monterey Sicilian fishers.

The proximity of other peoples in Monterey, both in neighborhoods and in the canneries, made community building based on ethnic solidarity far more difficult than if this group of Sicilian fishers interacted only with one another. Portuguese, Mexican, Spanish, and Asian peoples threatened the formation of an ethnic enclave of fishers by their very presence and participation in the fishing industry. While Sicilians used marriage to resolve conflicts over village and class among themselves, conflicts between Sicilians and their ethnic immigrant counterparts played out most obviously over the issue of marriage, or intermarriage. The issue of intermarriage with non-Sicilians came up in relation to questions about "conflict." The narrators' focus was on gender and generational conflict, usually over issues of access to wage work and personal freedom for girls. However, intermarriage was often the unintended outcome of the personal freedom brought about by wage work, and provided a glimpse into the extent that Sicilian immigrants expressed their sense of themselves as a community.

Campanilismo

The constant influx of immigrants who had direct connections to villages of origin reinforced a powerful sense of *campanilismo,* or village loyalty, for Monterey's Sicilians. In Sicily there was great attachment to one's village, and great rivalry between villages, many of which did not even have roads connecting one to another simply because "there was no reason to go there."[3] Fisherpeople were more isolated within their villages than Sicilians from agricultural regions, especially those who lived on islands such as Marettimo. Fishing cultures also tended to isolate rather than integrate fishers from the larger regional or national group.[4] In his study of San Francisco Italians, Dino Cinel noted that the fishermen among them "proved that . . . a group could isolate itself almost totally from the larger society, re-creating patterns of economic and social organization almost entirely from the Old World."[5]

People carried their attachments and prejudices with them in their migrations. The fact that they visited and revisited their home villages throughout their lives, and continued to receive relatives and friends from home, reinforced their attitudes about themselves and about one another, making the bridge to community in Monterey harder to build, but all the more important. Anita Ferrante described her allegiance to Marettimo as "tremendous": "You come from a village. It is united. You attach yourself. You become tight. I adore my village. When I see someone from my village my expression of love comes out to greet them on the streets of Monterey. It is wonderful. I ask about their aunts, uncles, cousins. We all know our families so well."[6] It was a great comfort to her and to others to be able to continue the village relationships in Monterey, but it had the dual effect of separating one group of Sicilians from another, challenging the idea of a Sicilian fishing community as one entity.

Migrants from Isola Della Femina and San Vito Lo Capo, who generally preceded the Marettimares in the Monterey migration, considered themselves "adventuresome," "the owners of the boats, the canneries," "businesspersons," "the entrepreneurs." Marettimares considered themselves harder workers than earlier migrants from San Vito Lo Capo or Isola Della Femina, by way of explaining their quicker acquisition of homes and property. Natives of Isola Della Femina and San Vito Lo Capo nicknamed the Marettimares "M&Ms" as a way of disparaging them. Marettimares, who tended to achieve middle-class status quickly, were resented by migrants from the other two villages. Some migrants dismissed differences owing to village origins: "It is no big deal. Some of my best friends are M&Ms."[7] More commonly, Marettimares were considered ostentatious: "They dress up, you know. You can always tell [that someone was from Marettimo] because they are showy," explained Katy Reina (pseudonym), whose family immigrated from Isola Della Femina.[8]

The Marettimares were perceived by other migrants to hold particularly tightly to the views that work in industrial canneries was inappropriate for women. Middle-class Marettimares generated resentment from female cannery workers who came from other villages. "No one looked down on us for working in the canneries except the M&Ms."[9]

The way Sicilians expressed difference along the lines of village of origin could be hurtful but were not serious impediments to the formation of community. One of the ways they overcame *campanilismo* was through marriages that connected families by blood. In the random sample of marriage licenses issued, most Sicilian-Sicilian partnerships connected people from different villages of origin.

Female Forms of Organization

The other critical form of community building and connection came through women's informal gatherings. Through these gatherings women came to know one another in a deep way, going beyond immediate family and village. Donna Gabaccia, in her work on gender and immigration *From the Other Side*, noted that this method of building community through casual neighborhood gatherings of women (and men) was common for many immigrant groups in the period of great immigration, 1820–1990.[10] As well, it was part of the "porch culture" of the working-class American South.[11] In Monterey, both women and men from Japanese, Portuguese, Spanish, and Mexican ethnic groups formed into clubs such as the Cervantes Spanish Lodge and the Aurora Club.

Sicilians went beyond formal organization, however. Sicilian women especially took the idea of informal gathering to a new level. It was a constant and requisite part of being a member of the community. It was often ritualistic, and exclusive, even to the point of excluding Italians not originally from Sicily. Women of other ethnicities also came together informally to strengthen friendship and build community, which had the effect of reinforcing ethnic differences in Monterey.

Rosary groups, for example, began to form in the late 1920s, exactly when marriage licenses reflected less intermarriage with non-Sicilians. Maria Mineo remembered her rosary group as consciously inclusive of Sicilian women from different villages: "We get together, say our rosary, then have a little coffee, cake, talk. . . . I like to have friends, people. *But these were not my people. They came from different directions, towns in Sicily, so it was hard to get close together.* But this way, we enjoy. Afterwards, we make a little shopping, spend the afternoon."[12]

Women in the rosary group arrived at the home of the week's hostess at a certain time. Prompt arrival was an important sign of respect. The rosary was said in unison, and a series of prayers followed, almost all dedicated to the Virgin Mary. Afterward, strong coffee and homemade dessert of cake and cookies, along with candy, were served, in much the same fashion as the embroidery groups. At this point, women physically removed themselves from the setting where the rosary and prayers had been said and created a space, usually around a kitchen table, where talk could be freer and more relaxed.

Women gossiped, laughed, engaged each other, matched wits, and teased each other. In the context of the group, now that the prayerful part of the gathering was finished and women sat comfortably around the kitchen table, they were free to express whatever what was on their minds at the moment. Everyone usually talked at once and conversation increasingly became loud, outrageous, even bawdy and silly. The talk seldom escalated into serious disagreements, although occasionally feelings would be hurt. If things got too disagreeable or serious, the group would disband and reorganize according to more congenial lines. Getting along was an essential part of rosary group if it was to accomplish the purpose of creating community.[13]

Sicilian women belonged, simultaneously, to rosary groups, sewing or embroidery groups, and even card-playing groups. Members of an embroidery group might gather on Tuesdays for the rosary, for example. There was a certain fluidity and inclusiveness about who belonged, just as there was a certain structure about the meeting itself. The only requirement was that one show up on a regular basis and take a turn at hosting the group, and that one was Sicilian; village of origin did not matter. Groups of friends and kinswomen came together to create practical art, to pray to the Virgin Mary, and to make a place for themselves in the city of Monterey. Their rich dialogue bound them together as Sicilian women, and at the same time increased their attachment to Monterey, just as other ethnic immigrants and high rates of intermarriage may have threatened their sense of identity and created hostility to the host environment.

Sicilian women also utilized their proximity on the cannery assembly lines to form bonds with one another and to overcome differences between families and villages of origin. At first glance, the narratives suggested a bonding in the workplace that mimicked camaraderie between workers in other contexts, and might have had the effect of bringing cannery women together as a self-conscious group. However, it was clear from the narratives that non-Sicilians were systematically excluded even from the togetherness of the working environment, and that the "closeness" Sicilians remembered was limited to a feeling of intimacy with other Sicilian workers. Nancy Mangiapane expressed Sicilian women's sense of friendship and understanding among one another: "There was a closeness. . . . My mother brought a big sack to work with fruits, vegetables, leftovers from the night before. We'd warm it on top of the pipes and we'd all have lunch together. . . . We looked out for each other. We had a lot of fun," she remembered.[14] "We used to walk to work together in the early morning hours over the railroad tracks. We'd follow the tracks together to work," as Esperanza Ventimiglia Ernandes recalled cannery work in the thirties.[15] By "we," Sicilian women meant each other, not their Portuguese, Japanese, Spanish, or Mexican neighbors and coworkers.

This is not to say that the exclusion was absolute. Cannery workers of all nationalities commented on friendship at work. "We made so many friends in the canneries, being with all those women," said cannery workers over and over again. "In the canneries everyone was one big family. Everyone was close. We ate together and made friends with everyone."[16] The friendships at work were superficial, however. Sicilian women formed a solid bloc on the job, and most important, when the workday concluded, so did the relationships between Sicilians and non-Sicilians. Non-Sicilian women were not included in the social and cultural gatherings, large or small, that Sicilian women organized around the idea of a Sicilian fishing community of Monterey.

The nature of fishing required the absence of husbands, sometimes for extended periods. This was not the case for most other ethnic cannery workers, whose husbands either worked in the canneries too or found other labor in Monterey and its outskirts. Even when husbands participated in fishing, such as the Portuguese and Japanese men, the women in these ethnic communities neither organized into a community of fishing people nor were they included in the casual gatherings of fishermen's wives that the Sicilian women participated in.

Sicilian women, on the other hand, went home from the canneries to do housework, but also to gather in communal sewing or embroidery groups, to talk together, eat together, and share their lives. With husbands often away on fishing trips, Sicilian women drew strength in the freedom they had, in ways that most working-class women in other places had neither the time nor the leisure for. "You couldn't talk much at work; you had to keep going. . . . But our husbands were never around. They would go to Alaska and they would stay three months. It was terrible, but it was great too. We needed a break [from them]. We had plenty of freedom. We'd meet every day and crochet or embroider while the children would play. We couldn't have done that if our husbands had been around. Your mind is at ease when you crochet."[17] Nancy Mangiapane explained, "My Albert was away fishing all year long, Alaska, San Pedro. . . . I had to keep up with the house, clean, take care of the kids, visit the family, work. But I didn't mind him going away so much because it was less work for me to do. You know how men are; you got to cook special. Across the street from me I had two girlfriends and we used to get together, even go to the show. It worked out nice."[18] From a child's perspective, it appeared to be only joyful: "Every afternoon, my mother, her cousins, her *commares*, would gather at Big Sarah's and have coffee. They would talk together, laugh, joke around. We were free. We took off and roamed the neighborhood. When we got hungry, we would stop at the closest house for lunch."[19] It was also obligatory. "We spent all of our time visiting, visiting, visiting people, bringing food, going to homes and them coming to see you," recalled Rose Marie Cutino Topper, whose parents migrated to Monterey in the 1930s from Isola Della Femina by way of Pittsburg.[20] It was this process of continuous small-group gatherings on the part of Sicilian women that formed the building blocks of a defined Sicilian fishing community. It was in these casual meetings that women decided everything from what to make for dinner to whose children ought to marry. "Women were in charge of everything. Our mothers used to cook, clean, do all the finances for the family. Then they would pack us all up and take us camping in Big Sur. We have all these pictures of the women in aprons scurrying around, putting up tents, doing everything. They made us all close. And we still are. Even today."[21]

The community bonding that women did during the periods when men were absent on fishing boats only intensified with men's return. During the period of the full moon, for example, sardines could not be fished because the fish were clever enough to see fishing boats in the moonlight and escape the nets. This presented an opportunity to bring men into the larger circle of the Sicilian community that women were in the process of creating. Cannery workers and fishermen of other ethnicities were not included in these celebrations of togetherness, even though they too were unable to work and might have been invited. The monthly parties celebrating fishermen's return with the full moon were exclusively Sicilian events, organized by Sicilian women. "It was a big celebration. . . . We had huge dinners [where] everyone contributed their favorite dishes, sausages, and card games where people would go from neighbor to neighbor for dessert and coffee. All the families got together, and everyone stayed up all night, fried sausage, then got up in the morning to go to church."[22]

Neighborhood and Class

Poverty was widespread among Sicilians in Monterey in the earliest years of settlement, from 1915 through the 1920s. Along with great poverty, several narrators described unmistakable class divisions among Sicilians early on, as boat owners separated themselves from workers, even within families. That difference played out socially and geographically. Boat owners and cannery owners lived above the wharf areas, while workers found homes along the wharf and in New Monterey. Even on occasions such as festivals and special events that were designed to bring the Monterey Sicilian community together in a meaningful way, people with capital separated themselves from those without. According to Mrs. Lucy Ventimiglia Gruwell:

> There were eight of us in the family. . . . Monterey was a one-horse town in those days. It was all dirt roads. There was no pavement. There was a big Italian community. They were very poor. In fact my mother used to have maybe a dime to her name at one time or another. And she'd buy a can of soup to feed us. . . . It was very hard. Money for sardines was very low. We gave my mother so much out of our paychecks. At times we were lucky to come home from school and share a can of beans. It was so bad. Those were real bad days. People lived from hand to mouth.
>
> The boat owners weren't poor. The Ferrantes and Eneas, Compagnos, I think. The ones that fished for them were. The poorer people like us lived along the wharf in New Monterey. Most of the workers in the cannery lived where we could walk to the canneries. There were canneries on the ocean side and warehouses on the other side. I worked in three or four canneries. The boat owners lived on up the hill from Pacific Street. We didn't socialize with them unless they were relatives, and even at that we weren't that close.[23]

Narrators stressed the importance of neighborhood as a class marker in their accounts of the landscape of Monterey, with poorer immigrants clustering close to the wharf areas where they could walk to work. According to Rosalie Ferrante, "You have to understand about the Italian community. There were layers. There was Uptown versus Downtown. Everyone was part of it and you knew where you fit by where you lived. And if your family owned a boat or a cannery or property."[24] The hills of Monterey became known as "Boat Owner's Hill," in the 1930s through the 1950s, indicating the strong Sicilian presence there, as well as the developing class divide, while the settlements in Pacific Grove and New Monterey were mostly working class.[25] Families indicated their status in the community by where they located their homes.

Many families who moved into the areas of Monterey above the wharf in the period between 1930 and 1960 were content with what they considered an adequate step up the economic ladder, and remain in the same homes in the present day. Many of their descendants accumulated enough wealth to move (and to move their parents) to upper-middle-class and wealthy neighborhoods in Pebble Beach, Carmel, Carmel Valley, and Monterey. The reluctance of immigrants now in their eighties and nineties to move beyond the boundaries of Monterey proper, regardless of changed financial circumstances, has something to do with age and reluctance to make transitions. However, it was a cultural reluctance as well, brought on by the sense that they were uncomfortable about any possible accusation that they thought they were better than anyone else, regardless of accumulation of money or property. In fact, they went to great lengths to demonstrate otherwise, and continually denied differences of status. "They did not want people to think they thought they were better," explained Peter Coniglio, a former mayor of Monterey.[26]

People who could not afford to move away from the wharf described conditions as difficult and expressed resentment about the status and gains of others. Phyllis Taormina grew up in the household of her grandmother on the wharf in the 1930s, along with her divorced mother and two brothers. The fact of her mother's divorce certainly affected the family's lack of economic well-being, but the grandparents lived close to the poverty line themselves, notwithstanding the addition of their daughter's family in the household. Mrs. Taormina's mother worked full time as a seamstress and turned over all her income to the grandmother. "My mother gave my grandmother every cent she made. She couldn't buy us nothing. I had no clothes, no shoes. We were really hungry." Mrs. Taormina was not only expected to do housework and child care, she also had to scavenge for food. "We were poor. I gathered mustard greens for our vegetable. Or I would sneak over and get a lettuce or carrot from my uncle Rico's garden when he was fishing." She resented Sicilians who moved into the middle class. "People made money here, but they didn't share or anything. They kept it to themselves. We didn't get no help from no one."[27] The fact that Mrs. Taormina expressed an expectation of help from other Sicilians, which was not forthcoming, suggested that Monterey's Sicilian fisherpeople understood that they belonged to one another and shared responsibility for one another in a special way based on a shared sense of identity.

Status was complicated further by family connections that brought together boat and cannery owners and workers in the same family, working for one another. For example, in the Nuovo family, one member owned a boat and employed his brothers-in-law, whose wives all worked in the canneries. Rose Nuovo, the boat owner's wife, did not do cannery work, as her sisters did. Everyone understood the economic and social disparity that came from the one couple, who were the owners of the boat, and the other members of the family, who were the workers. The extended family gathered at the boat owner's home each week to receive their shares of whatever the boat brought in. This was an indication of the "*respetto*" or deference traditionally given to boat owners. Still, the family was uncomfortable with growing economic differences among themselves. "There wasn't really this class thing. . . . Rose never, never, never lorded it over anybody. She was a good mother, a good, kind, very respectful person," said her sister, a former cannery worker.[28]

Sicilians in the present day, especially those from middle- and upper-middle-class families, hold on to the notion of the level playing field from the beginning of settlement in 1915. Mike Maiorana, whose family owned boats and now owns several businesses, argued, "Basically everybody that came here was poor. Everyone was on the same level. Then some people did better than other people. They made something of themselves. Nobody liked that. There were jealousies."[29]

Jealousies were brought on by real unfairness and bad luck. One fisherman, Erasmo Peraino (pseudonym), worked as a fisherman on other people's boats for many years, and finally bought a boat himself, but not until 1949, too late to yield much of a return on his investment. By then, the sardines had disappeared from Monterey Bay, and only those fishing families with significant capital and resources for travel to southern California, Alaska, and South America profited from fishing. Mr. Peraino recalled, "The season began on August 1, and as time went on there was more and more competition. There was big money to be made. Cannery owners were cheating the fishermen. San Carlos was owned by an Italian, and that was the worst. They would give you credit for four tons when you brought in nine. We hated that guy. I spit on his grave."[30]

And yet, the man in question, Angelo Lucido, owner of San Carlos Cannery and reviled in Mr. Peraino's (and others' narrative accounts), was also held in great esteem by Sicilians and considered an important member of the community despite his treatment of his compatriots. Mr. Peraino went on proudly to relate the following, widely known story about Mr. Lucido, suggesting more admiration than disdain: "No Italian, Black, or Jew could buy property in Pebble Beach. Angelo Lucido was the first. And then one day Mr. Samuel B. Morse himself wanted to borrow money, and Lucido made him wait three hours. Three hours. Then, 'send him in,' he said."[31] Sicilians held on to a notion of one community that embraced every Sicilian, in spite of differences of village or class, deep resentments, long memories, and outright feuding where members of the community were not on speaking terms with one another.

Dating, Marriage, Divorce: Challenging Boundaries

Class differences, like differences related to *campanilismo,* were not dealbreakers in terms of the formation of community for Monterey's Sicilians. Narrators expressed awareness of village origins as well as class consciousness, and at the same time, ambivalence about village and class. However, they were never perceived as fixed or even insurmountable barriers among and between Sicilian families, most of whom also identified as Sicilians and believed in the possibility of upward mobility, along with the majority of Italian immigrants elsewhere.[32] Barriers between families based on *campanilismo* and class could be surmounted by marriage, both formal and informal gatherings, through work on the fishing boats, and especially among women in the canneries. Sicilians intended to go further than merge with one another, however. They also meant to define their community apart from the rest of Monterey, even as they sought to appropriate the landscape of Monterey into something of their own.

The willingness of Sicilian parents, especially mothers, to bend with new realities such as dating and divorce, instead of remaining intransigent, kept the families together and the community intact in the face of change. Women used their power in their domain of the home to absorb the changes that were necessary in order to keep their families close and the community intact.

Women in families took charge over the behavior of women of younger generations and tended to ignore or tolerate the same behavior in their sons. They struggled with how much latitude they would accept and at what point they would demand conformity. Their decisions were rarely made in the privacy of nuclear families but extended to the circle of kin and *commares* that made up what was taking shape as a Sicilian community. Rose Enea recalled a network of Sicilian mothers who struggled with cultural conflict and decision making in the absence of husbands, who were usually away fishing but who generally relinquished power in the home to their wives: "When there was a dance or something that my [daughter] wanted to go to, I would call up all of my friends and we would sort of decide what to do together. If I asked my husband, he would say 'you decide.'"[33]

The fact that husbands were away fishing for such long periods of time intensified women's roles in the home and created conflict over appropriate gender roles for girls. The women in the Ferrante family were allowed by their mother to test some of the boundaries of female behavior. Pietro and Rose Ferrante migrated to Monterey in 1917. There were six daughters in the family, and no sons. Pietro was clearly the patriarch and noted for his success in the world of fishing, but it was Rose who arranged for a small amount of rebellion on the part of her daughters, without allowing them to break completely with the traditional patriarchy of Sicilian culture. It was a delicate negotiation on her part.

In 1934 Rose's sixteen-year-old daughter, Mary, wanted to work for wages in order to buy American clothes and makeup. Even though the family had the resources to provide her the luxuries she wanted, it was considered frivolous to allow daughters allowances for such things. Rose allowed her to go to work at the local Woolworth's, knowing that Pietro would disapprove. In fact, Pietro was never explicitly told about the job, although he was presumably aware of it. Soon thereafter, however, the teenager came home for lunch one day to find a young man sitting at the kitchen table. "Who is that?" Mary asked. "That is your fiancé," said her father. She ran to her room, sobbing, and had to be forced out. She married the boy, however, just as she was expected to do. It was the end of her rebellion. Her mother helped her in a limited way, and in doing so, perhaps kept her daughter from stronger measures. The daughter was satisfied to work for enough wages to buy little luxuries. She did not aim for full-scale independence, and her mother understood that.

The bonds of acceptable behavior were often challenged, but not broken. This story is an example of how Sicilian families, as individual units and as a community, absorbed change but were able to withstand any serious challenge to their hegemony over their children. Rose Ferrante quietly helped her daughter Mary do what the daughter was determined to do: find work and gain the limited independence an income would buy. The daughter wanted only a small thing. The mother allowed it. The father looked the other way. Together they saw to it that resistance would be limited to the little job at Woolworth's. Later, after her daughter married, her mother again quietly aided her, by offering temporary, but not permanent, refuge when her daughter faced difficult times in her marriage. Rose never allowed the daughter to challenge patriarchy completely. But she did allow her to push at the edges to alter things if she could and helped Mary reconcile herself to her situation if she could not.[34] Like Mexican families in the Central Valley, boys were allowed more freedom, and parents were more flexible with them in terms of dating and marriage. Both women and men struggled with gender roles under the twin pressures of being new arrivals as immigrants, and being poor.[35]

Mary Buffo remembered that girls were guarded carefully in Monterey Sicilian families: "They always had a hand over them [the girls]. The boys just had more freedom. That's the way it was. So they [parents] kind of expected boys to do that [date non-Sicilians] but not the girls. They tried to do everything they could to keep it from happening [to the girls]. They would yell, scream. Threats."[36]

Many families indicated great pride in their children's marriage partners if those choices were from Sicilian families. They showed an equally great disappointment when they were not. It was difficult enough to marry a Sicilian outside of the Monterey community, much more a non-Sicilian, even if the person was of Italian origin. The marriage of a Sicilian to someone of Anglo, Spanish, or Portuguese origins was at best greeted with serious concern and usually opposed as much as possible, in spite of the fact that it was relatively common. "It helped if the boy was Catholic. Spanish, Portuguese was much better [than Anglo or German]. They [Anglo or German non-Catholics] were just too different. The stronger aunts would talk to the daughter," explained Rose Marie Cutino Topper.[37] Lucy Ventimiglia Gruwell remembered her father's raised eyebrow when she told him her fiancé was Spanish rather than Sicilian. "But he [her husband] was Catholic so that was good. Easier."[38]

The acceptance of dating, and even of divorce, as long as it was within the bounds of the Sicilian ethnic group, showed incorporation of some aspects of American culture among Sicilians, even as they resisted assimilation into the American mainstream. Lorraine Fazzini's (pseudonym) family owned a cannery in Monterey, and she and her sisters worked in the cannery offices. Lorraine handled all the money as the accountant for the family firm. She not only worked for years but dated freely before marrying a Sicilian at the rather late (for the 1940s) age of twenty-six. "My mother supported me. She made sure I had a nice wedding and that I was invited [to baptisms, showers, social events]."[39] Despite the daughter's willingness to test the limits of moral behavior, her mother made sure she remained bound to the family and community by ignoring or accepting behavior that was not too radical. Lorraine might have tested the limits of proper behavior for girls but was protected by her willingness eventually to conform to ethnic imperatives by marrying a Sicilian man.

Josephine Vultaggio (pseudonym), whose parents had immigrated to Monterey in the earliest years of the sardines, explained: "In my mother's day [the 1920s], when the parents of the bride did not like [their daughter's suitor], they said, 'Get Out!', and that was the end of him. But it's not like that anymore. . . . My daughter fell in love with a real bum and we couldn't do anything. We yelled and cried. But she was in love. What can you do? We had to swallow our spit. They got married."[40] The marriage records suggested that parents had far less control over marriage partners in the 1920s than Mrs. Vultaggio remembered. In this particular case, the man in question may have been "a real bum" in terms of his character, but he was from one of the oldest and wealthiest Sicilian families in Monterey, while the Vultaggio's were working class.

It was not a happy marriage. The couple divorced after eleven difficult years, having had two children. "She finally had enough. I used to go visit her and see red marks on her face. I knew [he was hurting her]. But I couldn't do anything. I gave her money, food. My heart got smaller and smaller. Thank God she got a divorce." The daughter remarried and lives happily in Monterey with her husband, who is also the son of a prominent Sicilian fishing family.[41] In this way, class differences were overcome, and divorce was tolerable within the bounds of the Sicilian community.

Family violence was unusual among Sicilian immigrants in Monterey, who prided themselves on the warmth and closeness of family life. However, it did occur in families, and women in families decided how to manage it while keeping family and community intact. "God has seen enough," Mary Pagnini (pseudonym) decided after her daughter, Dorothy (pseudonym), fled to the mother's home for the third time. She was escaping the violence of her husband, who was later diagnosed with a mental illness. This mother helped her daughter obtain a divorce. In doing so, she made sure her daughter stayed close to the family and the community. The mother did not risk losing her daughter, either to the rage of the husband or to the anonymity of American life.[42] And yet, among fisherpeople, women's labor traditionally gave them personal freedom and independence of movement. The consequences of that traditional liberation challenged gender roles and community boundaries in Monterey.

The Castrucci family (pseudonym) is a good example of how wage labor brought out conflict over gender roles, and how family and community responses indicated that boundaries were being marked off by Sicilians in Monterey along lines that defined their community as ethnic fishers. This family arrived in Monterey in 1917 from Martinez, California. Lillian Castrucci Sanchez (pseudonym), born in 1918, was the youngest daughter in a family of four children. Now age seventy-eight, she recalled her reasons for quitting school in eighth grade after overhearing her parents' fretful conversations about the lack of money in the family:

> No one told me to. I just got the idea. I heard them talking in the kitchen. They were worried. I wanted to help them. I wanted to help my father keep his boat. So I quit school and I went to work cutting abalone on the wharf. I had to lie about my age and I didn't know what I was doing. But the other ladies, they were all Italian ladies, they said, "Give her a chance; we'll teach her how to do it." I loved the fresh air. I don't like being cooped up. It was hard work. But I was so happy to give that money to my mother. She never said a word. She never asked me why I wasn't going to school. She just took it.[43]

It showed exceptional enterprise and independence for a thirteen-year-old girl to quit school and go to work all on her own. Her response to the impending poverty in her family was not only positive, but also proactive, in the tradition of Sicilian women, and among female fishing people. Wage labor gave this young girl a striking amount of freedom of movement. She was not chaperoned, or even watched very closely, as long as she was perceived as contributing to the family finances. Her family needed her to work for a wage, and that required their letting go of control over her movements. In return, she turned over every penny to the family. "I got a paycheck and I would hand it over to my mother. The whole thing. I never thought of taking anything for myself," she said.[44]

She soon began dating, unbeknownst to her parents. "I was seeing this boy from Carmel. We would go to the beach." At age seventeen, Mrs. Castrucci Sanchez met her prospective husband, who was Mexican. She recalled meeting him secretly and going for drives (which involved heavy petting) in his uncle's car. Her older brother, who dated many non-Sicilian women with impunity, discovered her relationship and exposed the situation to the family. At this point, the family's interest in her suddenly kicked in. Her brother was dispatched to end the relationship. She decided to elope and, she thought, settle the matter.

Her elopement in 1935 created open conflict in the family, which spread to the community at large, making it clear that by this time there was an intact Sicilian community of fishers in Monterey. Mrs. Sanchez was ostracized for choosing a Mexican man as marriage partner. Her prior independence, ambition, and less-than-chaste behavior had been ignored because, at the time, she was making a critical contribution to the family income. Her marriage would end that contribution, of course. Had she chosen a Sicilian man from a respected family in Monterey, as her sisters did, the economic loss to the family might not have meant so much. Girls eventually grew up and got married and stopped adding to their family income. Everyone accepted that. Her choice of a Mexican man, without financial resources himself, threatened the cohesion of a community based on ethnic homogeny and fishing. Her family and community strenuously opposed her.

Mrs. Castrucci Sanchez remembered that her mother and sisters "never supported me, not one of them. They wouldn't visit me or anything. Here I spent years giving my mother my whole paycheck and she [her mother] turned her back on me." Punishment meant exclusion from afternoon visits with female relatives and their children, as well as from the large extended family and community dinners that defined social life for Sicilian families. Mrs. Castrucci Sanchez's isolation highlighted the fact that this was not a community in the making but a community formed, and one that was based on cooperation and mutual support. Her exclusion created great hardship for her. "My sister had people over. They [had been] my friends too. I knew them. But they never visited me [even though this woman and her husband lived in the same neighborhood as the sister]. They never invited me to nothing. I felt so bad all the time. I used to cry about it."

She did what she could to resist ostracism and to force inclusion. "I just brought my kids over and visited [her sisters] anyway," she said. When she and her husband went through a financial crisis of their own and became destitute, she demanded the help normally offered freely to grown daughters in financial trouble. "I said to my mother, 'You help me. You give me those rooms in the back' [an add-on apartment that was being used at the time by boarders]. And she did."

According to Mrs. Castrucci Sanchez, her husband, Luis, sought a fishing job on her father's boat. However, Mr. Castrucci refused to help him break into the fishing business, either by employing him or by asking another boat owner to employ him. This is something that continues to cause resentment because she and her husband were poor at the time, and really needed the income fishing would have brought. Mrs. Castrucci Sanchez remembered an incident when her brother-in-law needed labor and chose men waiting on the docks to help on his boat, pointedly ignoring his own brother-in-law, who was standing among them.

The family united to clarify boundaries concerning behavior. It was not acceptable to marry a man of Mexican descent. "They didn't like him because he wasn't Italian. That's all it was. That's why they acted so mean. Boy they were mean."[45] Marriage between a Sicilian and a Mexican or Asian person was beyond mere consternation. It was unthinkable, and yet, as the sample of marriage licenses suggested, also fairly widespread, at least in the years between 1906 and 1925. The fact that so much intermarriage occurred may have led to the deep-seated bigotry at work in the Sicilian community between Sicilians and Mexicans.

Racism and Community

Portuguese women and women who defined themselves as Spanish, not Mexican, emphasized the exclusivity of the Sicilians in the 1930s and 1940s. "We got along with the Italians at work, but afterwards, that was a different story. We're really European, not Mexican, and the Italians didn't notice that. They didn't bother with us, but most of my friends now are Italian," said Mary Longueria, eighty.[46] "Some of it was very nasty—what I heard," recalled Juanita Segovia, eighty-four. "The Italians were not like the Spanish people. They were very forward. We were calm, quiet. I remember my mother said to me, 'Juanita, I do not want you to become acquainted with the Italian people. They're mean."[47] Emily Rodriguez dated a Sicilian boy in 1941 and wanted to marry him. "This boy said, 'I really love you but you have to wait. My family doesn't like Spanish.'"[48]

It was not a smooth transition between the migrations of the 1920s and the Italian community of the 1970s. Much of the tension that shaped reconstructions of class and gender took place at home and within families, arenas in which women played vital roles. Sicilian families negotiated the conflicts among themselves, while struggling to create a strong sense of community based on their sense of themselves as fisherpeople connected by kinship, occupation, history, and ethnicity. "We did what we were supposed to do. I don't have no regrets," said Rose Davi.[49] "We were a kind of community apart," remembered Joe Sollecito. "It was the old story. Didn't assimilate. Stayed with our own group. Only talk[ed] Italian."[50] That sounds innocent enough, but it meant separation at the very least, and as narrators from outside the Sicilian community suggested, a sense of unfriendliness, even resentment or hostility, directed at anyone from outside the tight circle Sicilians created, especially if marriage was an issue.

The events of Pearl Harbor and the outbreak of war with Italy brought the issue of assimilation in all of its multiple forms into sharp focus. The Sicilian commitment to Monterey as home-site was tested. The forced and often permanent displacement of Japanese Americans brought out the worst in Sicilian attitudes about race and ethnicity. The temporary displacement of Sicilians led to new acculturation strategies, politically and socially. It was not enough to create community among themselves; Sicilians needed the security American citizenship brought. Gender differences counted too. Women more than men bore the brunt of forced relocations because so many women failed to become American citizens, and as a result were suspect in the eyes of the state.

4. Good Americans

It was a bittersweet time in the Italian community. We were the majority in town and we were a tight community. We were kept close and protected as kids. The main concern of the families was the boys in the service. There was a whole generation that went to war: the Mercurios, my cousin Tom, so many young men from Monterey. Most of them chose the navy. We were all patriotic. We kids collected tin foil, rubber, and participated in the Douglas MacArthur paper drives. I won a medal for the paper drive. We all wanted to help the war effort.

—Interview with Peter Cutino, August 31, 1998

We do not try to measure the loyalty of citizens, but we think we can know when they are traitors.

—Linda Kerber, *No Constitutional Right to Be Ladies: Women and the Obligations of Citizenship* (1998)

The desire to acquire citizenship on the part of new immigrants is a measure of the extent to which they express a sense of belonging to the body politic of their adopted state. As such, it is both a highly valued and highly controversial matter for immigrants, for their hosts, and for scholars of immigration. The issue of citizenship continues to divide scholars and policy makers.[1]

Not surprisingly, scholars interested in the issue of citizenship are from diverse fields of study. However, citizenship is gauged by political rather than economic or social behavior, and has attracted the special interest of scholars of politics.[2] Fishers, however, tended to be less political than workers in other industries.[3] Sicilians in Monterey were no exception. "My father really believed that Italians needed to have [political] power, but they weren't that interested in voting. They were fishermen," said Mary Brucia Darling, whose father Antonio Brucia, a bar-owner, sought to marshal Sicilian political power in Monterey, even before the controversies of World War II.[4] Mrs. Darling remembered the efforts of her father, who organized the Sons of Italy in 1928 as a political association. She explained: "My father believed in the vote, in citizenship. He was responsible for more than five hundred

Italians becoming American citizens. He filled out their citizenship papers, acted as their witness, and took them to the county court in Salinas to pass their test and take their oath."[5] The Sons of Italy remained a small entity, however, as they struggled with the political apathy of Sicilian migrant fishermen in the years before Pearl Harbor.

Context

No one listed as mayor, member of the city council, board of supervisors, sheriff's department, or any of the hastily organized citizens' defense groups in Monterey, Pacific Grove, or Pebble Beach had an Italian surname at the time of Pearl Harbor. Despite the economic predominance of Italians in the 1930s and 1940s, they had no political visibility whatsoever. This made them vulnerable to government action without the benefit of having anyone in a position of power who could influence policy or speak for them, even at the local level. Monterey as a whole was almost entirely focused on the production of sardines in the 1940s and included a disparate mix of ethnic and national groups. Working-class ethnic Montereyans generally were far more interested in labor issues than civics.[6]

Moreover, Sicilians in Monterey had no real memory of decent or fair government in Italy, which made them even less likely to become active politically.[7] Peter Coniglio summed up the general attitude: "They [Monterey Italians] would never consider complaining, much less making a major protest. They accepted authority, but they did not trust government. They had been so beaten down in Sicily by the government."[8] Joe Sollecito agreed: "Of course it wasn't right that we had to leave to go to Salinas, but you avoid trouble, conflicts [with authority], and you don't complain. That's it."[9]

The local newspaper, the *Monterey Peninsula Herald,* is an invaluable source as a measure of Monterey's political climate in the period from Pearl Harbor through the war years, particularly as supplement to the narrative interviews. I examined the local newspaper both for content and placement of news stories. Placement proved to be an important issue, especially in terms of defining apparent connections between local and national events.

Sicilians were rarely the subject of any news reports or stories prior to Pearl Harbor, but they were a decided focal point in the wake of the attack. In turn, Sicilians may have paid closer attention to events in Sicily and in Italy before the bombing of Pearl Harbor, but afterward, they showed an almost single-minded attention to local affairs. For example, though the *Monterey Herald* paid little attention to the rise of Benito Mussolini, Monterey Sicilians, who were otherwise apathetic about politics locally, were aware of

Italy's transformation under Mussolini and generally supported it. Mussolini appeared to be a strong leader who had a vision for Italy that would modernize, industrialize, and unify the country. Sicilian migrants felt especially hopeful for the changes Mussolini promised. "Most people thought he was a pretty good guy," recalled Albert Mangiapane, who immigrated to Monterey in 1925, three years after Mussolini came into power. "Some people were afraid of him because he made so many changes, but he brought law [to Sicily]," he said.[10] Others remembered their mothers sending wedding rings to the Italian government to support Mussolini's war effort. "Most [Monterey Sicilians] thought Mussolini was a hero," said Peter Cutino.[11]

Their attitudes and perspectives were shared with other Italian Americans during this period.[12] In an analysis of Italian experiences in California, Gloria Ricci Lothrup argued that the period between the two World Wars marked a time of renewed enthusiasm for Italian politics and culture among California Italians, who numbered 100,911 by 1940.[13] According to Lothrup, Mussolini himself made vigorous efforts to attract support among Italian American immigrants and was largely successful, especially in California. He actively encouraged everything from after-school Italian language programs for children, to political and economic associations connected to Italy, to cultural events and clubs, even sending his son on a friendship mission to California specifically.[14] Lothrup focused on the Los Angeles area, and emphasized a "new ethnic assertiveness" on the part of Italian American immigrants there in the decades of the 1920s and 1930s, in part a result of the power that the Mussolini regime represented for them.[15] This was expressed in increased membership in numerous organizations such as the Sons of Italy; a proliferation of Italian language newspapers and political tracts supporting fascism and the Mussolini regime; and even public affirmations of Mussolini by the Roman Catholic Church and the Italian Catholic Federation in California.[16]

Monterey Sicilians expressed their strong and continued attachment to events in Sicily and Italy as well. They affiliated equally with their original homes as well as their adopted one in Monterey. Their close and continued association with Italy only became problematic with the Italian invasion of Africa, and the subsequent joint invasion of France with Germany in 1940. These events caused concern among Monterey Sicilians, even as they were evidence of Italian power and a source of ethnic pride. They were afraid that the United States would be drawn into war with Italy. "We didn't want to see brothers fighting brothers," said Peter Cutino.[17]

It was also at this moment in time, 1940, when the first piece of national legislation was passed regarding aliens. The Alien Registration Act (the Smith

Act), signed into law in June 1940, required the registration and fingerprint-
ing of all aliens, age fourteen and older. Moreover, aliens had to fill out an
extensive questionnaire detailing their occupation, residence, marital status,
organizational affiliations, and means of entry into the United States.[18]

Pearl Harbor and Its Aftermath

Japanese immigrants in Monterey may have had less sense of communal
transnational identity in this period, according to political scientist David
Yamada, but as a group, they would bear the harshest consequences of policy when the Japanese military bombed Pearl Harbor on December 7, 1941.[19]
Soon afterward, the United States declared war on Italy as well as on Japan.
Sicilians remembered this as a catalytic moment in time: "When Italy went
to war against the United States, their faith in the Old Country was de-
stroyed," said Peter Cutino in reference to his parents and older relatives.
His mother, Rose, remembered the outbreak of hostilities between Italy and
the United States as a family issue: "Everybody had families [in Italy]. We
were torn and very, very sad. We were American but our heritage was there
[Italy]. People were disappointed. No one could get letters, packages, everything stopped. We didn't know what was happening to them. It made us feel
funny that Italy was at war with us."[20] Suddenly, the politics of control and
national security became paramount at the federal, state, and local levels and
forced Sicilians to reconsider everything about their behavior, their identity,
and their goals as a community.

The narratives reflected a sense that a climate of fear and chaos pervaded
Monterey, and newspaper accounts supported that view. Peter Cutino commented, "You have to understand that there was great, great fear that the
Japanese were going to land any minute. Everyone thought that the invasions
were going to happen. The Rocky Mountains were going to be the first line
of defense. People were really scared. I remember the fishermen were scared
to go out because there were sinkings along the coast. Then of course, they
couldn't go out. The government wouldn't let them. Then the government
began confiscating fishing boats to use to defend the coast. They confiscated
my uncle's boat."[21] Mr. Cutino's remembrance indicated his and other Sicilians' general assumption of an "us Americans" versus "the enemy Japanese"
attitude at the moment of Pearl Harbor. Even though Italy was part of the
Axis alliance, many Sicilians were not American citizens, and Sicilians in
Monterey had created a separate, almost closed community.

Newspaper headlines alerted Monterey residents to preparations against
such an attack: "Army on the Alert to Defend Pacific Shore," began one such

piece. "After months of training ... soldiers ... stand guard from Canada to California to defend this country from possible attack by the Japanese."[22] Curfews, blackouts, and air raid drills were implemented. On December 10, 1941, Mayor E. G. McMenamin posted a notice declaring "A State of Emergency to Exist in Monterey," expanding the powers of "Air, Police and Fire Wardens," and that a policy would be enforced that limited the movements of all residents. The mayor and city council announced ominously that "all enemy aliens are to be watched,"[23] which caused enormous anxiety among Sicilians. They published legal notices from time to time throughout the war announcing "expanded powers" for themselves and reminded residents of proper behavior during imposed blackouts.

A state of emergency was proclaimed for the state of California by the governor, Cuthbert Olson, on December 15. "There was definite danger of air attack by planes in the immediate vicinity. . . . Flares were seen in the sky, apparently dropped by enemy aircraft," explained an army communiqué. The governor announced, "This state may at any time become a theater of war, [and] placed in effect the emergency orders of the state council of defense governing individual activity throughout California."[24] Air raid warnings added to a general atmosphere of tension and confusion as Monterey prepared to be the next point of invasion and bombing.[25] "Scores of residents who peered out of darkened windows [as a result of emergency blackouts] noticed troops along the waterfront standing alert against any eventuality."[26]

Though the German presence remained small and dispersed in California generally and Monterey specifically, the Japanese and Italians formed visible communities, something they had never considered to be anything but a positive, even a strengthening attribute of their settlement process. However, on January 25, 1942, the Roberts Commission, headed by Supreme Court Justice Owen J. Roberts, issued a report that charged Japanese Americans living in Hawaii with complicity in the assault on Pearl Harbor, thus igniting a public outcry. Suddenly, any member of an ethnic group that was part of the Axis Powers—anyone of Italian, German, or Japanese descent—was suspect as part of a fifth column.[27] "California is wide open to any kind of fifth column activity," said then–Attorney General Earl Warren to a meeting of one hundred sheriffs and district attorneys in San Francisco: "All who have read the [Roberts] report on the Pearl Harbor attack must realize we have a tremendous problem in California to protect the state against fifth column activities . . . a definite part of Axis warfare is a widespread use of spies and well-organized sabotage."[28] Californians saw themselves as on the front lines of the war effort in terms of action against "enemy aliens," as well as on the front lines of production while a burgeoning defense industry advanced quickly to combat the threat.[29] The enemy aliens Californians were worried about were Italians and Germans as well as Japanese.

The FBI launched raids against suspected members of the fifth column in the weeks following Pearl Harbor and throughout the war. One such raid took place in February 1942. "It was the most extensive series of raids yet conducted by the federal men in their drive to suppress fifth column sabotage and espionage activities. Members of secret German, Italian and Japanese societies were included in the days round-up . . . [including three Italian men from Monterey] identified as members of an Italian organization said to have fostered a fascist program in this country."[30]

The first order of business was the strict enforcement of the California Alien Land Act, which prohibited Japanese nationals from land ownership. Widespread arrests of enemy aliens followed. Although 222 Italians were arrested nationally by December 20, this is in stark contrast to the 110,000 Japanese Americans who were systematically rounded up and sent to concentration camps in the Midwest.

Enemy Aliens

Recent scholarly analyses of Pearl Harbor and its aftermath have repeatedly emphasized the extent to which the Roosevelt administration directed its propaganda campaigns against the Japanese, even though many Germans and Italians would be included under the umbrella term "enemy alien." Racial representations of the "enemy" in popular culture—films such as *Tora Tora Tora* and *Victory at Sea*, for example—focused entirely on the Japanese.[31] Monterey Italians shared this sense of racism against the Japanese in their midst. "The only thing we felt bad about was why did we have to move out of town? The Italians didn't do nothing. We didn't hurt nobody. It was the Japs that did it," said Nancy Mangiapane.[32] Gaetano Rossetti (pseudonym) reflected on the sudden removals of Japanese Americans and admitted to the pervasiveness of thinking that everyone of Japanese descent shared guilt over Pearl Harbor: "There was this Japanese kid who sat next to me in school, and one day he was gone. I didn't care. The truth is we all sort of said good riddance . . . of course we felt kind of bad for them, but we thought, 'hey, they deserved it.' "[33]

Sicilians were focused on their own situation, not on the far worse plight of the Japanese, in spite of the fact that many Japanese shared a common bond with Sicilians in the fishing industry. For example, in an interview with one narrator who was part of the forced evacuation of Monterey, Gaspar Aliotti, the Japanese internment is a far less important part of his story than his and his family's short-term relocation. He found work in the construction of an assembly center for Japanese who would later be relocated to concentration camps in the Midwest for the duration of the war, not just for the short term:

> I was more or less still on a honeymoon. The war was started and my wife and our newborn son were all living with joy, with a new home and a start of our family life. Then an order from our government to evacuate Italian noncitizens from the coast of Monterey at this time. My wife was not a U.S. citizen, so we had to prepare to move. You can imagine the heartbreak of leaving our new house to comply with the request of our government to move. We had to rent our home and leave. We went to live in Salinas. It was not easy. As I started to look for work and asked if I was of Italian descent. I was turned down every time although I was a natural-born American. This was very disturbing. After combing the city of Salinas for work, I finally found employment at the Salinas Fair Grounds. I went to work as a carpenter. We were building a prison camp for interned Japanese and worked there for a time until the project was finished, [and] after a period of time we were able to come back to Monterey."[34]

It did not matter so much in peacetime that one did not have official citizenship papers, but it suddenly became a crucial distinction with the advent of war. Sicilians who lived in Monterey for decades were suddenly considered "dangerous nationals" because they lacked official citizenship. Some believed they were targeted because of their ethnicity, rather than their inability or unwillingness to obtain the requisite qualifications for citizenship. "Some people don't like Italians," said Rose Davi by way of explanation for the forced removals.[35] However, they were careful to avoid claiming ethnicity in the public sphere. Sicilians quickly grasped the danger of making ethnicity the issue rather than citizenship. The official focus for Sicilians in Monterey was on citizenship. "We had to become naturalized American citizens. . . so that this couldn't happen to us again," said Mary Anne Aliotti, discounting the Japanese experience.[36]

Compliance, Race, and Evacuation

In Monterey, so-called "enemy aliens" were not allowed to fish or to work in the canneries. Newspaper articles assured Monterey citizens that fishing would continue without enemy aliens: "Federal regulations . . . include provisions that . . . all fishing boats must be manned by American citizens only."[37] At the same time, "Japanese [were] barred from fishing" without regard for citizenship criteria, and "Italians and Slavs are now the chief fishermen."[38]

The subsequent focus of Monterey Sicilians on the issue of citizenship rather than ethnicity or race suggested that newspaper articles such as this might have indicated to them that though the Japanese were regarded as a racial group, there was a chance that they might be considered differently. The citizens among them might be treated as such, and only the noncitizens would suffer the consequences of enemy alien status. Sicilians actively pursued a "possessive investment in whiteness" that they hoped would inoculate them from the politics of exclusion facing the Japanese.[39] They responded as most Japanese responded, with compliance rather than resistance to the order to evacuate and to the humiliations of being connected to the Axis by ethnicity. However, Sicilians seized the issue of citizenship as a means of redefining themselves as a community that would unequivocally be American in terms of political identity. The Spadaro family was forcibly relocated to Salinas during the war, but responded by donating the family fishing boat, *The Marettimo,* to the war effort. Giuseppe Spadaro announced that "I wanted to give the boat because I have no sons to send the army."[40]

The Japanese attempted to do the same. The Japanese-American Citizens League (JACL), formed in 1929, helped organize the 442d Regimental Combat Team to fight in the war on the American side. A "culture of compliance" on the part of Japanese Americans was documented in films from the concentration camps, narratives, and pledges of allegiance to the U.S. government.[41] However, the Japanese were hampered by racial restrictions on naturalized citizenship. According to U.S. naturalization law, Asians were explicitly excluded from naturalization.[42] This was amended during the war years to include American allies—China, the Philippines, and India—whose citizens could become naturalized American citizens after 1946. On the other hand, while Italians were socially regarded as nonwhite throughout the early years of the twentieth century, they qualified as "white" legally, which allowed them to become naturalized American citizens.[43]

Rogers M. Smith's critical analysis of the history of citizenship makes a compelling case that American citizenship has always been connected to race, gender, and religion, rather than liberal ideals that came out of democratic values or the Enlightenment.[44] Literature on citizenship and constructions of whiteness demonstrated that "becoming white" was both an ever-changing process and an essential factor in gaining basic civil rights, including the right of naturalized citizenship.[45] Linda K. Kerber's seminal work on citizenship and gender demonstrated how the rights, responsibilities, and obligations of citizenship were limited for women generally, immigrants and nonimmigrants alike, and only corrected systematically by legal challenges over the past two hundred years.[46] The experiences of Japanese Americans, as well as many thousands of Germans and Italians nation-wide, demonstrated that ethnicity and race continued to influence definitions of citizenship, particularly in times of national crisis. People who were le-gally citizens of the United States (both naturalized and by birth), who were home owners and business owners, were not immune to persecution by the American people or prosecution by the United States government. Emer-gency measures enacted by the Justice Department during World War II justified everything from searches and seizures to arrests and imprisonments. Moreover, while Jews, Slavs, and Italians were legally "white," they were "denied a full share in whiteness itself" by native elites, including those in Monterey, who viewed southern European immigrants as uncultured folk well into the middle decades of the twentieth century.[47] The United States government appeared frightening and omnipotent, and American people arrogant and arbitrary, to Monterey Sicilians during World War II.

It began to look more like a fatal error than a simple oversight to have neglected so obvious a statement of loyalty to the United States as the acqui-sition of official citizenship. In the months after Pearl Harbor, there was a flurry of activity, and conflicting information reflected both in the pages of the local newspaper and in the narratives that made it imperative for Sicilians as "suspect ethnics" to make their political allegiance clear, as well as to as-sume a place in the dominant population.

Sicilians did not pursue a strategy of organized resistance, perhaps because all of a sudden they did not want to draw undue attention to themselves as different ethnically or racially. They felt bombarded by haphazard policy, however, and it was difficult to respond to the many actions directed against enemy aliens generally. Enemy aliens had to register their presence. Several were arrested. Property was seized by the FBI: "The government prepared today to seize a billion dollars of enemy alien assets as collateral for any American claims against the hostile governments, and a special force of G-men was ready to impound the enemy-owned property."[48] There were seri-ous penalties for any enemy alien who tried to hide property considered contraband by the United States government: "The justice department issued a warning today that any Japanese, German or Italian national found in possession of a camera, regardless of the use to which it is put, faces loss of his equipment and possible detention along with 'dangerous' Axis nationals in concentration camps. These aliens—more than 1,100,000 in all—also are forbidden to possess firearms."[49]

The first order of forced evacuation of enemy aliens occurred on January 29, 1942. It was followed on February 19 with Executive Order No. 9066, signed by President Roosevelt, that allowed the military full discretion in evacuating the coast of anyone considered an enemy alien, citizen or not. It was this order that added a level of complexity to the situation for Sicilians in Monterey. Few families were immune, because most had at least one member who was a noncitizen enemy alien. "It would be difficult to find a person of Italian ancestry in this region [Monterey] who has no relatives affected by the . . . order. And in most cases Italian-American families face a choice of being moved as a group, because the mother or father is an alien—or establishing two homes, one inside and one outside the 'prohibited' zone."[50]

As the deadline for evacuation approached, numerous articles in the newspaper documented the process. "The present evacuation was ordered by the department of justice; now the army is in charge. The original order covered enemy aliens living within 100 designated areas in California, Oregon, and Washington. With its new power, the army if it wishes can sweep the state clean of not only enemy aliens but their American-born children as well."[51]

Churches and schools within restricted areas were closed to aliens.[52] "It was a regular exodus [out of Monterey]," remembered Betty Lucido, as Sicilian families moved to San Jose, Gilroy, Morgan Hill, and Salinas in the months following Pearl Harbor.[53] The numbers varied, but "best estimates with those close to the situation indicate about 600 aliens of Italian nationality actually will be forced to move [out of Monterey], taking their families with them for a total evacuation of perhaps more than 1,400."[54] The inclusion of American citizens—specifically, children of enemy aliens—in the order to remove enemy aliens from the coast created confusion and anxiety among the Sicilians in Monterey as well as among the Japanese. Vincent Bruno recalled this climate of uncertainty: "Rumors were flying . . . no one knew where they stood or what they were supposed to do."[55]

Newspaper articles warned of arrests and imprisonment for those enemy aliens who failed to register or comply with all restrictions. In a piece headlined "Advice for Enemy Aliens," one writer cautioned that "It should be borne in mind . . . that the federal government has spoken and that there will be 'no exceptions' whatever. Therefore, it behooves every 'enemy alien' no matter how long he has been an 'American' in everything but formal citizenship, to learn what is expected and comply."[56] No one wanted to put themselves or their families at risk, but many were confused about what was expected of them, and who exactly fell under the umbrella definition of "enemy alien." "A brief check-up by the Herald revealed today . . . that the people most concerned—those who must leave their homes and in many cases their families, are willing to do whatever the government suggests. What they now want more than anything else is definite instructions on what is expected of them."[57] Sicilians were fearful that issues of citizenship were being confused with issues of race and ethnicity regarding the logistical problem of the forced migrations out of Monterey. Sicilians in Monterey understood and respected how bad it must have looked to American society and the American government that so many of them had not acquired citizenship, and they wanted to be perceived as Americans in the context of the war.

Sicilians reacted with shock and disbelief to the registrations, property seizures, and expulsions, but also demonstrated a lack of understanding for what constituted genuine citizenship. "Nobody could believe what was going on. My father almost had a heart attack," remembered John Mercurio.[58] "We were shocked," recalled Rose Aiello Cutino. "We didn't know what was going on. The Italian people had always been so good, no police, we never got in trouble. We were scared. To tell you the truth most Italian people were afraid of their own shadow. Everyone was a good citizen. We got along wonderful with the Americans here. It [the removal] was very, very sad and terrible. People took it real hard. It hurt," she said.[59] It had come as a shock to Sicilian fisherpeople that lack of participation in politics, beginning with the fundamental act of acquiring citizenship, would have such a powerful impact on their status in the Monterey community.

Gender and Citizenship

For Sicilians in Monterey, particularly women, acquiring legal citizenship was a detail in the process of migration that was often overlooked. Citizenship was regarded as a trivial legal nicety, or just assumed. Joe Favazza described his mother, Providenza, as a "good American": "She loved America. She was devoted to the United States. She didn't even give her ring to Mussolini when everybody else did. She was a good citizen even though she didn't have her papers."[60] According to one local observer, "Among the Italians, there are a great many families in which one of the adults, usually a husband, has become a citizen while his wife remains an alien. Because of the new restrictions, the entire family . . . will move."[61] Rosalie Ferrante supported that observation from personal experience: "The ones who had to leave were the noncitizen grandmothers, so the whole family went too."[62]

Women who were called "enemy aliens" of the United States often had several children to care for. They spent their days cooking, cleaning, and working in the fish canneries. Many were illiterate in Italian, and spoke little English. Therefore, it was often considered understandable for women to fail to make the time to attend school or learn English, much less pass challenging citizenship tests in front of judges. Giovanna "Jenny" Costanza's father had become a naturalized citizen, but like so many other families, her mother did not: "My mother felt it was humiliating to have the judge ask you all kinds of questions, and she wouldn't do it."[63] When women did acquire citizenship, it was considered remarkable rather than reasonable. Catherine Lococo, who was in her twenties during the war years, proudly related her mother's efforts at acquiring citizenship in spite of the obstacles of daily life: "My mother worked hard. My father had a lot of relatives. She cooked and cleaned for them and she had eight children. I always think of her by the stove. My mother was exceptional. Her parents wouldn't allow her to go to school as a child, so after she was married she was determined to become a citizen. She was in her forties when she went to Mrs. Tice's classes a block away from where she lived. By Pearl Harbor she was a citizen. We were so proud of her. She was an amazing woman."[64]

Even as they found increasingly public spaces for themselves in the environment that they created in Monterey, Sicilian women remained focused on their own community, venturing out of their homes to work in the canneries or to participate in the social and family events. Mike Maiorana recalled, "There were six of us kids. My mother got together with the other women in the neighborhood to say the rosary once a week. She helped with the church, the *festas*, Santa Rosalia. Other than that she was a homebody. My father became a citizen, but she never did. She made sure all of us were educated, though. She never wanted to go back to Italy. She came here to stay and that was it. She never thought that would make her into an enemy."[65]

Men who had not become citizens were considered "lazy" or "stupid" by others in the Sicilian community, in contrast to women, who seemed helpless and victimized. Peter Cutino recalled a clear distinction made between men who were citizens and men who were not: "The ones they moved were noncitizens. I remember my uncle laughing at them [fishermen the uncle worked with] because they hadn't bothered to get their papers and now look what happened to them. He said, 'Serves them right.' They should have taken the time, made the effort, you know, to get their papers."[66] In contrast, Mary Anne Aliotti summed up the general attitude toward noncitizen women: "Poor thing. What was she going to do? How could she have done that [become a citizen] with all the work, the children?"[67]

Catherine Lococo had only been married a year when the war broke out. She had moved from Monterey to live with her in-laws in San Diego. She had almost refused to marry her husband because he had never become a citizen. Sicilian women were aware of the interconnections between gender and race that adversely affected citizenship. At a symposium on the war years in Monterey, Mrs. Lococo commented, "There was this law that if you married an alien you became an alien too. It was so unfair."[68] Still, Mrs. Lococo commented on her husband's reluctance to acquire citizenship in the prewar years as a matter of his own irresponsibility and lack of foresight:

> It just wasn't that important to him[before the war]. . . . If you were an alien like my husband you had to be inside by 8 o'clock. He was frightened to miss his curfew. One night we were late coming home from a movie and we ran. I thought, why am I running? I'm American born. I'm not doing anything wrong. But he suffered for it [lack of citizenship]. He became very, very depressed. He couldn't get a job. When you went for a job they would say, "Are you a native born? Are you an American citizen?" That's when you had to say the truth: "No I am not," he would have to say. "I'm an alien." Maybe they would hire him for a day but that was it.[69]

Her narrative expressed both the stress and shame on the part of Sicilian women and men when they realized their predicament as enemy aliens in a country at war with their country of origin. At the same time, she and others experienced confusion over their status as both a legal citizen, "American born," and also a suspect, a woman married to an enemy alien.

Gender and Class

Sicilians quickly realized that they had to engage actively in politics at the local level in order to assuage American fears about their loyalty as an ethnic group. Elite men in Monterey's Sicilian community played a crucial, public role in the effort to define issues. These were men who owned a stake in the economic infrastructure and were American citizens themselves. They ably manipulated the local media in their effort to demonstrate that Sicilian fisherpeople were loyal American citizens. They emphasized that as fisherpeople, they were essential to the local and national economies, and at the same time, that they were part of white American culture, that there was no question their political loyalty remained with the American government.

These Sicilian men, from the moment of Pearl Harbor, made public displays of loyalty and support for the government, and they demanded media attention. In the immediate aftermath of Pearl Harbor, sixty of Monterey's most prominent boat owners made a collective $50,000 contribution to the war effort and sent FDR a telegram, a copy of which was also sent to the local newspaper, reporting that "members of our group delivered six 80 foot diesel fishing boats to the U.S. Navy. . . . The balance of the fishing fleet here awaits the orders of the commander-in-chief. Carry on Mr. President and God Bless you! We are all behind you!" It was signed by the president of the Monterey Sardine Industries Association of Boat Owners, A. N. Lucido.[70]

Boat owners pledged $60,000. Common fishermen also raised funds to buy bonds and support the war effort. It was all front-page news in the *Monterey Herald*, placed next to a story that sardine fishing would resume soon, but without enemy aliens. Clearances to fish were issued as soon as boat owners could "prove that they have a crew composed exclusively of American citizens. No aliens will fish out of Monterey."[71] This had the effect of making clear that Sicilians considered themselves Americans politically, and were even willing to disassociate themselves publicly from those members of their tight community who were noncitizens.

The newspaper regularly ran photos and stories about local young men who joined the armed services. Sicilian men who enlisted were featured often. One such article showed a photograph of Salvatore Lucido, headlined, "Gotta Help My Brother." Lucido was identified as a "young Monterey fisherman." He was shown "completing purchase of $300 worth of National Defense Bonds from Louis Vidoroni, manager of Monterey County Trust and Savings Bank." The piece went on to reveal that this sum constituted "most of the young man's savings as a fisherman in his father's . . . purse seiner. . . . His brother, Thomas V. Lucido, is in the field artillery . . . stationed in Wyoming. Decision to purchase the bonds came after hearing President Roosevelt's recent address . . . the senior Lucido says with pride, 'It was the kid's own idea.'"[72] Though the individuals featured here were definitely Sicilian fisherpeople, they were, at the same time, portrayed as loyal American citizens who supported the war effort as combatants, as taxpayers, and as people who went out of their way to buy bonds and teach their children American values. The Lucidos were among the wealthiest and most prominent families in Monterey. They owned large purse seine boats and a cannery. There were no such comparable articles for families of Japanese, or for that matter of German, descent.

For elites, especially for men, one of the most important strategies in dealing with the perceived threat to themselves as an ethnic group was political involvement. Sicilian fishermen formed unions and politically oriented organizations in the 1940s and 1950s, during and following World War II. "In the forties Italians realized we needed some power. My father and his friends said, 'We need some clout.' That's when they ran one of their own, Shedo 'Buck' Russo, for mayor and Horse Mercurio for councilman," recounted Jack Russo.[73] In the aftermath of World War II, Antonio Brucia worked to impress on local politicians the importance of Sicilians as a political force: "When there were elections in Monterey, he would approach the candidates and pull out his 'black book' with the names of the five hundred citizens and ask the candidate what he would do for the Italian fishermen in exchange for their vote. In this way, he was able to have the city buy a fire boat in case a fishing boat caught on fire, have an Italian (Frank Marinello) put on the police force so he could act as interpreter. My father helped elect a councilman (Shedo 'Buck' Russo) who later became mayor [of Monterey]. He formed the local Sons of Italy Lodge [chartered February 5, 1950], and became its first president."[74]

Since that time, several Sicilian men won political office. There were several mayors and councilmen from the Sicilian community in the wake of World War II. In addition, many sons from prominent families turned to law rather than fishing as a profession, and became politically active. One second-generation son, Peter Coniglio, who later became mayor of Monterey, recalled his migrant father's encouragement to get a good education after World War II: "My father said, 'I don't want you to even get a taste of it [fishing].' He wanted me to go to school, to become a businessman, a lawyer, a teacher, to assimilate."[75]

Women, on the other hand, actively participated in organized public displays celebrating Sicilian culture and the culture of fishing as a way of connecting to one another and building a community of Sicilian fishing people in Monterey. Their efforts at community building were suspended during the period of the evacuations and the war. "We didn't want to make a big thing about it [Santa Rosalia celebration] with the war going on and all that. It was bad enough that everyone had to go to Salinas," explained Jenny Russo, referring to the forced evacuations of the coast. "We just couldn't do it [the *festas* and traditional group social events]. We were trying to keep the families together and to keep our homes—one home here one in San Jose. Everyone was afraid," she recalled.[76]

There were virtually no articles about public patriotism on the part of Sicilian women similar to those highlighting the efforts of Sicilian men, although there were several articles about elite Anglo women who made contributions of money and volunteer work to the war effort. Buying war bonds and donating property were not described as family contributions when they came from Sicilians, but rather gifts from particular men. Sicilian women from elite families appeared only rarely in the society pages of the newspapers. The one event that got public attention was the annual Italian dinner put on by the San Carlos Catholic Church Mother's Club. Otherwise, Sicilian women did not appear in the pages of the newspaper during the war years, in contrast to the men of their group, who were interviewed and reported on frequently.[77]

The absence of publicity did not mean that women remained inactive, however. Like the Japanese, they coped with the strains of war by acquiescence.[78] They complied with everything, from FBI raids to forced evacuations. Mike Maiorana, who was a child during this period, remembered the way his mother coped with the stress of the war years. His mother was not a citizen, and the family was subject to periodic raids by the FBI. There was no question of resistance. "The FBI confiscated our radio. My mother treasured that radio. She cried over it [after the FBI left]. It was a big piece of furniture. There were periodic inspections throughout the war. The FBI would come. They would show up unexpectedly and look through closets, drawers, cupboards. We had nothing to hide. My mother would say, 'I think it's about time for them to show up again.' And sure enough, there they were. It was uncomfortable for us."[79] Mr. Maiorana remembered that it was uncomfortable. It must have been unnerving for his mother. She was a recent immigrant who spoke little English. She needed amazing fortitude to cope with armed FBI agents searching her home without warning while her husband was away fishing. She had to deal with this intimidating situation alone, and also help her children manage the stress and humiliation of it.

Fishing and the War Effort: Placing Stories in the News

By the time of Pearl Harbor there was awareness that the ban on enemy aliens in the fishing and canning industry might affect fishing adversely, at a time when there was a critical need for canned protein: "[Monterey] has lost more than a quarter of its experienced fishermen. As enemy aliens, 2,234 of the 8,750 licensed fishermen no longer are allowed to put out to sea."[80] The newspapers carried stories on the sardine industry and its indispensability to victory for the Allies: "Canned sardines—popularized by World War I—are definitely going to play their part on the menu of fighting men, throughout the world, in World War II."[81] Front-page articles quoted both state and federal officials who "stressed the importance of U.S. Fishing fleets," and announced "Fish Vital to War Effort."[82]

There was a great deal of concern in the wake of Pearl Harbor that fishermen and canners, frightened by their questionable status as enemy aliens and the Coast Guard ban on fishing of any sort, would simply leave the area. "Sardine Season is NOT Over Here," a front-page story in the *Monterey*

Herald proclaimed on December 12, 1941, a few days after Pearl Harbor. "Far from it . . . purse seine fishing boats are being 'cleared' for resumption of work as quickly as possible. 'Some of them could go out tonight if they wanted to,'" announced W. W. Wyatt, who spoke for the U.S. Coast Guard as customs collector. "Meanwhile . . . the A.F. of L. cannery workers union were doing everything in their power . . . to resume the war time job of turning out food for this and other nations. . . . The world need for nourishing food—in compact packages—means . . . Monterey canneries will be operated . . . on as big a scale as possible."[83]

The placement of news articles was as critically revealing as their content. Reports on the status of both enemy aliens and sardines were almost always front-page news, placed next to the latest war news. It was odd to see headlines such as the following: "Alien Raids Continuing" next to "Catch of Sardines Landed" next to "Doomed Singapore Still Fighting."[84] A front-page story announcing the arrest of 2,500 "Axis Nationals" was placed adjacent to a story on the status of the "Sardine Fleet," and next to that a story on the "German Invasion of Russia . . . and Turkey."[85] Alongside a story on FDR's latest speech that the war threatened "U.S. Shores," a story was placed "Prob[ing the] Alien Situation," adjacent to which ran an article about authorizing two "Sardine Plants [to be built at] Moss Landing."[86] A piece about arrests of "fifth columnists" ran side by side with another about a record catch of sardines.[87] In fact, it was rare to find any articles about sardine fishing that stood alone, without some mention of "enemy aliens" or the evacuations or vice versa.

It may have been just coincidence that articles about "enemy aliens" and the forced evacuations were almost always placed contiguous to articles about the sardine industry. Yet, it was difficult to miss the fact that so many of the same people were involved in both. It may be argued that if Sicilians sought to distance themselves as an ethnic group from the roundups of enemy aliens, this would not be the way to do it. Those pieces linked them and identified them, as an ethnic group, to "enemy aliens." Conversely, if Sicilians wanted to show evidence of their contribution to the economy of Monterey in spite of the presence of large numbers of noncitizens among them, there was no better way. Everyone knew that "Monterey's important fishing industry was developed for the most part by men of Italian ancestry."[88]

Whatever the forces behind those editorial decisions, anyone reading the newspaper after Pearl Harbor certainly understood that Sicilians were essential to the sardine industry, that sardine fishing and canning was critical not only to the economy of Monterey but to winning the war, and also that Sicilians were included in the umbrella term "enemy alien." Their distinc-

tiveness as a group separated them from the mainstream, even as they struggled for inclusion. Elites, notably elite men among them, worked to temper
ethnic difference with public displays of patriotism.

Return

On Columbus Day, October 12, 1942, FDR rescinded the evacuation order
for Italian immigrants based on a recommendation by Attorney General
Frances Biddle. Italians were able to return to their homes after a six-month
removal. The narratives differed widely about the severity of the disruption
in their lives. Their age at the time of the evacuations affected narrators'
sense of loss and pain.[89] Generally, both women and men minimized the
experiences.

Sicilians usually shrugged off the policy of removals as normal aspects of
being at war. "We had to move to San Francisco and close up our house [in
Monterey]. We lived with my husband's uncle. It was only for three months.
It wasn't too bad. Then we could go home," remembered Vita Crivello Davi.[90]
Her sentiments were echoed by many others who ended a short explanation
of their experiences as refugees from Monterey with, "It wasn't so bad," or
"What are you going to do? It was a war. We just accepted it."[91] Mary Anne
Aliotti remembered her mother's stoicism and acceptance of government
policy, which gave the children a sense that there was nothing particularly
discriminating about their treatment:

> My birthday is on December the 8th. When I was 5 years old on the 7th, my
> father came home and said, "The Japs bombed us. Now what are we going to
> do?" They still gave me a birthday party. We were aliens. My parents were not
> citizens. First we were sent to San Jose, then San Francisco. My father went to
> work in the shipyards. It didn't make sense. He could have been fishing in
> Monterey just as well. But my mother just said, "This is life. We'll do the best
> we can." My parents came here for a better life and never regretted it. My
> mother made us feel as safe and as comfortable as she could. She protected us
> from feeling like aliens. We played outside. We went to school. We were even
> given money to buy savings bonds at school. Somehow some way they under-
> stood they were in a better country and they weren't going to complain no
> matter what the government did. And they didn't talk about it after that.[92]

The prevailing attitude among Sicilians was resignation and acceptance:
"My mother-in-law was really upset, but we never dwelled on it. We never
talked about it. She had twelve children, two in the service. For the most part
they [the government] left everybody alone. It came and went so fast," re-

ported Josephine Favazza, whose mother-in-law (the only member of the family who was not a citizen) had to move temporarily to Salinas.[93] As a result, the entire family moved with her. It would have been unthinkable to allow the mother to relocate by herself. Her son concurred that his mother accepted the evacuations without confronting issues of fairness or racism, even though this man joined the army during World War II: "She didn't say too much about it. It happened. Okay, you go on. She worried a little bit about losing her property because she was an alien. But she thought that whatever the government did was okay with her."[94]

Catherine Lococo recalled that she and her parents were part of the evacuation because her father, as well as her husband, had not acquired citizenship, but at the same time, she minimized her loss or trauma as part of the family survival strategy: "Everything turned out okay. I never heard my father or my mother complain about it. This was something they had to do. They were very conscientious people. My father was able to go back to work as a fisherman. They didn't lose any property. They prospered and got larger boats. The government never took our boats. There was no bitterness in my family."[95]

The Lucido family had migrated to Monterey from Vito Lo Capo in Sicily in 1935. The entire family, except the mother, became citizens. "After the Pearl Harbor, my mother had to leave [Monterey]. But we just had to go to Salinas, so it wasn't so bad. And we were all together. We thought [the policy] was stupid, but we just followed whatever they [the government] said. Afterwards, we came back. It wasn't a big thing to us," said Ray Lucido.[96]

When Sicilians were allowed to return to Monterey, they picked up where they left off, grateful that they were no longer regarded as political enemies by the rest of the community. Rose Marie Cutino Topper explained, "Most Italian mothers would never complain. My mother was so happy when she came back [from Salinas]. She kept saying, 'I'm so glad I'm back! I'm so glad!' And that was the end of it. They [her parents] didn't like to bring it up again. Soon the war was over . . . and everything was okay again."[97]

Mike Maiorana remembered the outbreak of World War II and the forced evacuations. His family had to move to Salinas for a short time. However, they did not question the policy or alter their feelings about their migration. "My parents were never bitter. They simply accepted it. It was just an experience. They were wonderful people and they went along with it. You showed respect to everybody, especially authority."[98]

Beyond just moving into normalcy, Sicilians struggled to acquire citizenship after their return, and also to blend a little better into the mainstream culture. "After the war, everything changed. It became really important to a lot of people to get their citizenship papers. They wanted to become Americans. And they wanted those papers. They thought that if something like this happened again, then if they had their papers they couldn't be sent out of the house. But that wasn't true. A lot of the Japanese were born here and they were sent to camps. It was terrible. My parents never got their papers. They were too old," said Ray Lucido.[99]

Joe Cardinale remembered his and his compatriots' determination in acquiring citizenship as soon as they could after the war: "I remember as soon as they got back to Monterey they went to citizenship school at Mr. Coletto's. He had a church on Pacific Street. Episcopal, I think. He gave classes in the back. Italians flocked to it during the war. It meant a lot to be a citizen. They followed the rules to the T. They didn't want to make waves or draw too much attention. They were scared they would be deported. But they also felt like the government was good. They knew they were in a war and they let this [the relocations] go because it was part of war."[100]

The issue of citizenship forced Sicilians to come to terms with their political identity. It was problematic to create a tightly knit community of ethnic fishers with so little sense of political affiliation in their adopted nation-state. Socially and culturally, women who came of age in the 1940s and 1950s emphasized the dramatic change the war wrought in terms of acceptance of intermarriage. They suggested that marriage with non-Sicilians was suddenly welcomed as a means of assuring community acceptance. "Before the war we only married inside of the community. It was terrible to marry a non-Italian then. But after the war that all changed. Everybody married everybody," said Giovanna "Jenny" Costanza.[101] The records of marriage licenses issued do not quite support that contention. The Sicilian community remained closely knit, and marriages within the Sicilian community circle of families were still the norm. The dramatic rates of intermarriage have occurred mainly in the past thirty years. Still, the perception on the part of Monterey Sicilians that there was a new acceptance of outsiders into Sicilian families in the postwar years is important, and this suggested that while behavior may not have changed, attitudes may have. Postwar Sicilians may have begun to appreciate that there might be significant advantages to acculturation into the larger community of Monterey, which included an American political identity.

Revising the Narrative

Beginning in the 1970s Italians, like the Japanese, began to rethink their own narratives of the war years. The Japanese critiqued the strategy of compliance within their community and challenged the United States government to make amends for its treatment of them.[102] Unlike the Japanese experiences, which were systematically documented in textbooks, films, and other forms of popular culture, Italian losses were not acknowledged at all until quite recently. This is not to say that Italians equated their own experiences with the far worse treatment inflicted on the Japanese, but that most Americans were unaware that Italians experienced anything like arrests, seizures of property, or loss of civil rights during the period following Pearl Harbor.

In recent years, Italian American citizens and scholars have made efforts to address the issue of the arrests, internment, and forced relocations of Italians during the war years. *Una Storia Segreta,* edited by Lawrence DiStasi, and *The Unknown Internment,* by Stephen Fox, are two products of the recent research focusing on the experiences of Italians in California, including Sicilians from Monterey.[103] This work challenged the United States government to admit to the arrests, internment, and relocations of Italian American citizens, as well as seizures of property. The emphasis in these accounts was on "U.S. residents and naturalized citizens" as victims of xenophobia and racism. Italians were victims: "If immigration itself constitutes a little death, then wartime for many Italian immigrants, and their communities, may come to be seen as yet another,"[104] argued Lawrence DiStasi.

DiStasi's collection of essays focusing on the war years emphasized the injustice for Italians, especially pointing out the hypocrisy of persecuting people whose children were actively fighting: "One San Francisco resident who had to leave his home . . . was the father of a service man killed at Pearl Harbor. In Santa Cruz, Steve Ghio came home on leave from the Navy to find the houses in his neighborhood boarded up. He could not find his parents or relatives."[105] *Una Storia Segreta* included anecdotes about excluded Italians taken away on stretchers, mothers and grandmothers torn away from their homes and children, and innocent people ruined financially and emotionally by the experience. "Were such people a threat? Were lives disrupted to any good purpose?" asked DiStasi.[106]

Stephen Fox collected extensive oral histories from northern California Italians about their wartime experiences as enemy aliens, emphasizing the extensive loss of property and disruption of lives that the evacuation orders caused families. Most Italians, like Monterey Sicilians, counted themselves fortunate to be spared the permanent and far worse treatment suffered by the Japanese. Still, Fox's wide-ranging and vivid collection of oral histories of people who were forced to evacuate the coast even for short periods, who lost property, and who experienced great anguish at the removals is an important part of the history of World War II in America.[107] His work demonstrated a new willingness on the part of Italians in general to call attention to themselves as an ethnic group by the 1970s. Moreover, the active participation of Monterey Sicilians in Fox's oral history project showed just how far they have come from a general attitude of blending in and moving on that overtook them during the war years, and how they have come to terms with the complexities of acculturation in the last two decades. Their stories reflected both a sense of pride in themselves as a ethnic fishing community and an equally strong sense of pride in their identity as American citizens.

There are some indications, however, of yet another shift in Sicilian attitudes about acquiring American citizenship. The passage of the 1965 Immigration and Naturalization Act effectively ended the quota system and encouraged family reunification. Sicilians took advantage of the new policy just as other immigrant communities did. Sicilians who migrated in the aftermath of the policy changes had no memory of the dislocations of the World War II years and no fear of exclusion. Immigration policy in the 1970s, 1980s, and 1990s reflected a geographical focus on Southeast Asia, Latin America, and the Caribbean, and a policy emphasis on illegal workers, refugees, and asylum seekers. As members of the European Union and part of the First World, Sicilian immigrants enjoyed a sense of themselves as welcome immigrants. In fact, as Italy became a destination as well as a sending country in these years, Sicilian migrants to Monterey shared many of the policy concerns that Americans expressed in legislation like the Immigration Reform and Control Act (IRCA, 1980) and Proposition 187 in California (1994).

September 11 only reinforced that view. As an ally of the Bush administration, Italy was a privileged member in the war on terror. Sicilians in Monterey were no more troubled by the legislation of 2001, the USA Patriot Act, than other American citizens, whether they actually acquired citizenship or not. JoAnn Mineo, age fifty-four, migrated to Monterey from Trapani in 1970 when she was seventeen years old. Mrs. Mineo married into a Sicilian family in Monterey originally from Marettimo, and has spent the past thirty years of her migration traveling to and from Sicily and Monterey. When asked about acquiring citizenship after so many years in the United States, Mrs. Mineo, like other postwar migrants, was emphatic: "No, no—I don't have citizenship. When do I have time? I have to work. It is not that important to me. It wouldn't change anything. I have my green card, so this is enough. I love America. I love Sicily too. Both."

Yet, sixty years ago, Sicilians in Monterey came to a conscious decision about who they were as a result of their experiences as ethnics and enemy aliens during World War II. Their experience of alienation during the war years stimulated an urge to connect with the American state as citizens. They began to construct an ethnic identity that actively bridged both communities but was based on American citizenship. Sicilian women continued a critical aspect of the process of migration and settlement interrupted by the crisis of war. Prior to the war, they had created public celebrations of ethnicity and fishing in Monterey that connected them to one another and to their roots in Sicily. Afterward, that celebration, the Santa Rosalia *Festa,* made a more explicit connection to the environment of Monterey and encapsulated all that was important about acculturation for them.

5. Women on Parade: The Political Meaning of the *Festa*

I don't know what they [his mother and her sisters] did. Crocheted, I guess. We were too busy fishing. . . . I don't think those women ever left the house.
—Interview with Peter Cutino, August 4, 1994

I was just a little girl. I remember being taken down to Cannery Row and being surprised. We went to my grandfather's cannery and it was so weird. There was no one around and it was always so busy. It was empty of men. There were no men anywhere, no trucks; no work going on. It was only women, all women—housewives. I remember being really confused by this. My mother dressed me as an angel, and we got to wear lipstick, and then I was on a float.

You know, that was the first time I saw women in charge—in control of everything. They were lining up, giving directions. They never went out of the house. But for this, they were out there, marching. It was women on parade! My Nonna [grandmother] was dressed in a white gown with a matching hat. It was so fun to see my grandmother out of the house, without her apron, directing people. . . . She told people where to line up, what to do. It was strange and exciting. The boats were work boats. But on Santa Rosalia they were all decorated. It was like Disneyland.

The important thing about this *festa*, this event, was the feeling, you know, the ambiance of the Italian community. It was all about community. After the blessing of the boats, everyone gathered in the piazza for a huge picnic. We kids went from table to table, eating, listening to the grown-ups talk. You ate what you wanted. If a stranger came, someone would say, "Here, sit down have a glass of wine, eat." People were like that—warm, close. There was a closeness, a spirit. The church was involved, yes, but it was really a fishermen's festival, not a religious thing in those days [the 1950s and 1960s]. . . . It really was a celebration. A "thank you" to Santa Rosalia, even if you didn't have such a good year, because your kids were alive, you could eat, that was enough to celebrate. It was a total celebration, a feeling of general contentment.
—Interview with Rosalie Ferrante, September 10, 1994

Rosalie Ferrante's vivid memory of the Santa Rosalia *Festa* in the preceding narrative suggested just how compelling a celebration it was in the eyes of a young child. By the 1950s and 1960s, when Ms. Ferrante experienced her first *festas*, there was a widespread perception among Sicilians and non-Sicilians alike in Monterey that the Santa Rosalia parade and *festa* represented both the Sicilian community and something important about Monterey history and culture. It did not start out that way, however. The Santa Rosalia *Festa* began as an effort on the part of Sicilian women to bring the Sicilian community together as fishers. There was a strong religious purpose about it in the beginning, and less concern about the broader Monterey community.

After the World War II years, and especially as fishing declined in the 1950s, Santa Rosalia changed in both focus and form into a public statement of Sicilian pride in explicitly connecting the Sicilians to the greater community of Monterey and to the economic history of fishing. At the same time, the *festa* remained the single most important identity marker for Sicilian fisherpeople and, as such, is the critical analytical focal point for understanding the multiple meanings of assimilation for them.

Scholars of ethnicity pay close attention to the ways in which ethnic immigrants do, and do not, express their respective identities. Micaela di Leonardo argued that women's nurturing, family-centered behavior defined them as ethnic Italian for the mainstream in California, and for one another. Furthermore, according to di Leonardo, Italian women found opportunities to express their ethnicity through celebration, mainly through food prepared during holidays. Their cooking and baking skills made them "authentic" in the eyes of family and community in important ways.[1] Unsurprisingly, Italian women who acculturated into a more conventional American life did not always continue their foremothers' traditional, labor-intensive cooking and baking, and felt some ambivalence about their own ethnicity as a result.[2]

This was not the case for Monterey's Sicilian women. In Monterey, Sicilian women fused ethnic identity with an identity as fishers. This worked to maintain a sense of self and community, even as Sicilians bent to the intense pressure to acculturate into the mainstream after World War II. The public celebration of the Santa Rosalia *Festa*, more than anything else, demonstrated exactly how Sicilian women made acculturation happen in complex ways for themselves and their families.

History of the *Festa*

Sicilian women in Monterey, like female fishing people in other times and places, shouldered many burdens single-handedly and simultaneously. When men went fishing, women were left alone to cope with everything from children, households, and extended families to the FBI searches and relocations during the war years. Children got sick or were disobedient; the plumbing or electricity went out; financial crises arose; feuds broke out among kin and between families. In addition, most working-class Sicilian women performed wage work in canneries. One of the ways women in fishing communities managed multiple stresses and crises was through prayer and ritual.[3] Sicilian women in Monterey prayed to Santa Rosalia, Palermo, Sicily's patron saint of fishing, to heal their children, keep men in their families safe at sea, restore bonds between estranged family members, bring about world peace, and end communism.[4]

As the legend goes, sometime in the Middle Ages, approximately 1100, Santa Rosalia, a young girl from the aristocracy, renounced worldly goods to live in a cave as a religious recluse, where she subsequently died. A peasant discovered her bones in a desperate attempt to restore his sick wife to health in the wake of a plague that had afflicted the town of Palermo. He was told, in a vision, to carry the bones of the soon-to-be saint through the town and give her a proper burial. In return, God would take his life in place of his wife's. He did so. The plague left the town (but he died). Thereafter, Santa Rosalia was worshipped as the patron saint of Palermo. Palermo was the major Sicilian metropolitan center for the fisherpeople on the western coast, and the saint was connected in their minds to the protection of fisherpeople from this region.

Many miracles at sea in the waters surrounding Palermo were attributed to the intervention of Santa Rosalia, who came to be associated with the safety of fishermen and their families. Migrants from Palermo (and vicinity) who had settled in Pittsburg, California, brought the *festa* with them. It was here, in 1934, that Francesca Giamona of Monterey witnessed the Sicilian celebration of Santa Rosalia on American soil, and was inspired to hold one like it in Monterey.

Santa Rosalia appealed to Sicilians in Monterey for the same reasons that fisherpeople in other cultures and other regions of the world practice certain ritual celebrations. Fishing is a uniquely hazardous occupation. Fishermen are always at risk in thousands of ways and dependent on the whim of nature and gods to bring them safely home. They cling to any possible talisman in their efforts to relieve the extreme anxiety their chosen livelihood brings them.[5]

Sicilian women prayed privately to Santa Rosalia, but they also went beyond the privacy of their homes and came together in rosary groups, which formed the building blocks of a Sicilian fishing community in Monterey.[6] Groups of friends and kinswomen came together to create practical art, to pray to the Virgin Mary, and to make a place for themselves in the city of Monterey. Their rich dialogue not only bound them together, it allowed for a free flow of ideas that led to all sorts of innovations that served both to increase their attachment to Monterey and to deepen their cultural roots. Sicilian women formulated plans for both the Santa Rosalia and St. Joseph's *Festas* during ritualized rosary group gatherings that moved them beyond the orbit of private spaces and led them to make a public event out of their private acts of devotion. Their public celebration of the *festa* brought wholeness and healing to a community of immigrants strained by everything from the nature of their livelihoods as fisherpeople and the process of migration and settlement to perceptions of bigotry directed at them and their families, especially in the wake of World War II. Eventually, however, men joined the process and connected the *festa* to the political and economic community of Monterey. This effectively required Monterey to include Sicilian experiences and culture in its mainstream history. By means of public displays of economic abundance interwoven with devotion to saints, Sicilian women (and later, men) proclaimed that the immigrant Sicilian fishing community in Monterey valued hard work, sobriety, thrift, and family, which conformed to traditional American middle-class values.

Scholarship on Italian community experiences in eastern industrial cities showed that public celebrations of special saints there did not have the same outcome. In fact, the almost pagan nature of the *festa* was treated with disdain by Anglo-Americans, other Catholic migrant groups such as the Irish and Germans, and the Catholic Church hierarchy.[7] However, Sicilians in Monterey dominated the two main Catholic parishes, San Carlos and St. Angela's, to such an extent that their traditional *festas* and events were produced and accepted as a matter of course, even as other ethnic groups such as Mexicans and Portuguese were systematically excluded from participation in those Sicilian *festas*.

The Portuguese created their own symbol of cultural identity in Monterey. The IDES, *Irmandade do Divino Espirito Santo,* or Brotherhood of the Divine Holy Spirit, was organized in 1889 by Portuguese immigrants from the Azores in San Jose and San Francisco, and spread to chapters throughout California during the 1900s, including Monterey. The IDES served the Portuguese community of Monterey in much the same way the Italian Catholic Federation (ICF) and the Sons of Italy served Sicilians. It was the focus of ethnic identity, culture, and social gathering. Unlike the Sicilian organizations, however, the IDES did not incorporate fishing culture into its version of Portuguese ethnic identity. Although many Portuguese participated actively in the fishing industry, they did not re-create anything like a culture of fishing people in Monterey. The IDES public *festa* celebrating Portuguese ethnic identity and culture, *Festa do Espirito Santo*, the Festival of the Holy Ghost, had nothing to do with fishing.

The Festival of the Holy Ghost, held the seventh Sunday after Easter, recalled a famine in the thirteenth century, when Queen Isabella of Portugal prayed to the Holy Ghost to help her people, and promised to build a church dedicated to the Holy Ghost if the famine would end. Two days later, ships miraculously appeared, laden with food. During the celebration that followed, the queen presented a young peasant girl with her crown, and built the church as promised.

The Portuguese celebration of the Holy Ghost in Monterey always included the crowning of a queen, in commemoration of Queen Isabella's thirteenth-century gesture, and also included a Mass, a parade, and a public barbecue. However, the Festival of the Holy Ghost never gained the prominence that Santa Rosalia eventually did. It did not go beyond the boundaries of the Portuguese community in terms of size, media attention, or political inclusiveness.

The Japanese community, recovering slowly after World War II, continued to form clubs celebrating various aspects of Japanese culture but never identified wholly as a fishing community. Although Japanese traditions and culture remain part of Monterey history, they have not commanded attention in the same way the Sicilians have.

On the other hand, Hispanic culture is deeply embedded in the history of Monterey. However, it is celebrated in the past tense, with a strong emphasis on the nineteenth century. The Monterey Museum of History and Art and the Monterey Museum of Art frequently engage the community at large in discussion, art, artifacts, and geographical remembrances of Monterey in the Native American and Spanish colonial periods, reaching back to the seventeenth century. However, at present a vibrant, activist Hispanic (particularly Mexican) culture is linked economically to agriculture, not fishing, and is celebrated in the streets of Salinas, Gonzales, Watsonville, Greenfield, and King City rather than in Monterey. Over the past fifty years, Monterey has definitively identified itself as a "fishing town" and is claimed by Sicilian fishing people as their own.

Origins

I interviewed several women who organized the *festa* in the pre–World War II years, then those who did so in the 1970s. Throughout the 1990s, I participated in the planning of the *festa* in order to gain an understanding of its beginning as well as how it has changed over time. Jenny Russo and Angie Bruno were impatient with my repeated efforts to understand the history and meaning of the Santa Rosalia *Festa* for Monterey's Sicilian community in the pre–World War II years: "Of course we were building a community here," Mrs. Russo insisted. "We wanted to have something for ourselves. It was in the 1930s, 1931, when we started the ICF and 1935 when we started the Santa Rosalia *Festa*. The fishing was good and we were all doing good. We wanted to be together, like family. It was all Italian—only Italian. The Santa Rosalia festival represented that. The real meaning of the *festa*, for us, in being Italian, was religious. We didn't allow divorcees to join the ICF, only married couples. But it didn't matter if you were Sicilian, Genovese, Neapolitan. We wanted to make a social group of Italians in the church. We would gather for a little dessert, coffee, a little dancing, a little singing. It was nice for us."[8] That assessment of inclusiveness was not supported by narrators who were Italian but non-Sicilian, and was a sore point for the non-Sicilian Italian immigrants who settled in Monterey. Theresa Canepa, whose family emigrated from Genoa and who later became a Monterey city councilwoman, commented, "If you were not Sicilian, you were an outsider. I was never in the parade. I never got to be an angel or a princess. That was for the Sicilian girls."[9]

In 1935 Francesca Giamona, Rosa Ferrante, Giovanna Balbo, and Domenica Enea got together in their rosary group and decided to celebrate the Santa Rosalia *Festa*, exactly as it was done as a traditional fall celebration in Sicilian fishing villages.[10] "The Santa Rosalia festival got started with three or four ladies from the ICF. They wanted to do something to honor her. She was the patron saint of fishermen, and Monterey was, after all, a fishing town. We brought her out every year on her day, which was about the 4th of September. We wanted to do it on the full moon so the men could participate too. It was very solemn, very special.[11]

Sicilian women focused on linking fishing with religion and ethnic community. Their primary goal was to create a ritual space where Sicilians from different points of origin could come together as one community of fishers around the common symbol of Santa Rosalia. Sicilian women firmly and confidently asserted their vision of Monterey. It was, for them, a Sicilian fishing town, enough like the villages they and their families left in Sicily to warrant the same traditional celebrations. Yet their characterization of Monterey as "a fishing town" was important, because much of the rest of the native population saw Monterey differently, at least in the 1930s and 1940s, in spite of obvious evidence to the contrary.

The newspapers once again offered a clue to the political and social climate of the broad culture of mainstream Monterey. In 1937 a popular local magazine, *What's Doing*, mentioned the Santa Rosalia festival in its back pages, but the widely read, only major newspaper, the *Monterey Herald*, ignored it. In a small, one-paragraph article titled "New and Old Festivals," *What's Doing* magazine explained that Mexican fiestas, Italian American feast days, and American festivals such as the Fourth of July have much in common, but feast days are distinguished for their religious overtones and tend to be "set apart for their solemn, sacred character." The writer described the Santa Rosalia *Festa* in two sentences as follows: "Of the groups comprising the population of the Monterey Peninsula, those of Italian-American ancestry have observed many feast-days, brought with them all the traditional, colorful celebrations of their native Sicily. All of which brings us to the feast of Santa Rosalia, that will be celebrated Sunday, September 16th."[12]

In 1940 William D'Avee, a Carmel writer, made the following observation in *What's Doing* titled, "Monterey and the Canned Sardine": "Monterey has three major sources of income: the fisheries, the tourist trade and the armed forces. Its attitude toward the first of these is little short of neurotic. To say that Monterey is 'proud' of its major industry is misleading. The pride of Monterey in the sardine industry is a far cry from the pride, say, of Pittsburgh in the steel business or Detroit in its autos. It is an industrial development of which an ordinary community would be very proud. It is a development of which Monterey seems scarcely aware." D'Avee's observation indicated that Sicilian women were correct in their understanding of the need for some acknowledgment by the larger community of Monterey that "Monterey, was, after all, a fishing town," that Sicilian working-class immigrants contributed enormously to the economic well-being of Monterey.[13]

Yet Sicilian women were hampered by restrictions on their social and political participation. Many spoke little English, were poor, and were not even American citizens, much less voters. There was little they could do to force acceptance on a population determined to ignore them. The celebration of the *festa*, however, was a perfect response. In their celebration of the *festa*, Sicilian women showed that they disregarded the generalized prejudice against fishing, and also against working-class Italian immigrants. At the same time, the celebration of the *festa* was a declaration of the political, economic, social, and cultural significance of their presence in Monterey.

The idea of a public celebration of Santa Rosalia spread from rosary group to rosary group throughout the Sicilian neighborhoods of Monterey. Women were delegated to approach Sicilian boat owners, cannery owners, and businessmen for help in raising money for the event. Although it would have

normally been inappropriate for women to solicit businessmen, religion gave
them a respectable, acceptable reason to organize and work publicly. They
also organized themselves into sewing groups and cooking groups to make
costumes and prepare the banquet that would follow the procession and
religious service.[14]

Women recalled the early days of the *festa* with a reverence for its piety
and simplicity. It was richly spiritual and at the same time, authentically
Sicilian. In the 1930s and 1940s the *festa* included the entire Sicilian community, and the essential nature of the event was woman-centered. Men
remained on the periphery, as supporters. There were no representatives
from local Italian social organizations in the early years. The *festa* participants
demonstrated values such as family, work, and religious devotion, all in the
context of the culture of fishing. They celebrated fishing and the Sicilian
people as integral to the political, social, and economic life of Monterey.

The planning for the *festa* traditionally began about two months in advance. Sicilian women in the Italian Catholic Federation worked with the
Carmelite nuns to make beautiful banners to be carried in the procession.
The women and sisters made a living rosary that the women of the ICF carried from San Carlos Church to the wharf for the blessing of the boats. They
used corks (representing the fishing industry) and made crepe paper roses.
They sewed a plain brown dress for a wooden representation of Santa Rosalia, with a crown of roses on her head. She would be carried on the shoulders of their husband fishermen in tribute on the feast day, exactly as she
was carried in Palermo and the villages.

Sicilian women organized little girls (always of Sicilian ancestry) to be
angels, and chose one of their daughters each year to represent Santa Rosalia, dressing her in traditional brown dress, garlands, and cross. "Women
picked the angels and queen, which was a competitive thing," recalled Catherine Lococo. She remembered long hours of "sewing costumes, decorating
the church, the floats, planning and cooking the community feast."[15] Once
again, however, only Sicilian women participated in this preparation in the
earliest years of the *festa*. Theresa Canepa recalled, "We were always reminded that we were not Sicilian. My mother was never invited to sew costumes
or bake with the Sicilian women."[16]

On the day of the *festa*, the entire Italian community gathered at San
Carlos Church for High Mass, which was said in a mixture of Italian and
Latin, and included incense, singing, and the saying of the rosary. It sometimes had to be held outside, in the church school's playground area, in
order to accommodate the crowd. Families then went home for a few hours
of lunch and rest before returning to the church to say a special rosary in

honor of the saint. They gathered at 2 o'clock and started the procession, which was held from San Carlos Church down one of Monterey's main streets, Abrego Street in the 1930s, to Fisherman's Wharf.

The band from Pittsburg came first, followed by the local parish priest with the altar boys. The girl representing Santa Rosalia came next. "I had to be Santa Rosalia every year until 1941 when the war broke out, and we stopped the *festa* for those years," remembered Josephine Giamona Weber. "I didn't want to do it; I was shy. But my mother made me. In the end I always gave in to her. It was important to her."[17] Three fishermen followed the young girl, carrying the wooden statue of Santa Rosalia on their shoulders.

The women came next. Fifty to one hundred women were dressed in long white gowns. They wore yellow satin neckties and white caps, as they solemnly carried the living rosary. The yellow and white represented the colors of the ICF. "They were so proud, so beautiful," remembered Catherine Cardinale, whose mother marched in the parade.[18] The rest of the community followed. The procession slowly made its way down Abrego Street to the wharf, where the priest blessed each fishing boat in turn, in the name of the saint. A wreath commemorating all the fishermen who had died at sea that year was thrown out onto the water, accompanied by prayer and solemnity. Afterward, the people walked to Parish Hall, where Italian desserts and coffee, made by the community of women, were served. Eventually tables were set up on the beach by the wharf. Everyone brought their pasta and bread and fried fish. Everything was shared, including the homemade wine.[19]

The *festa* not only reinforced a vision of identity as ethnic fishers for Monterey's Sicilian women, it also gave new migrants an opportunity to come together with Sicilian Americans and assimilate into their new community. In Marettimo, Santa Rosalia is not celebrated with the same intensity as it is in the other villages. Marettimares in Monterey seemed different in other ways, too. They were treated with a mixture of admiration and resentment for their economic enterprise and success.

The Santa Rosalia *Festa* helped to overcome those feelings of jealousy and division by allowing everyone of Sicilian ancestry an opportunity to work together in common cause. It was a defining moment for Vitina Spadaro, who came to America in 1937 from Marettimo:

> I was eight years old, just a little girl, when I arrived in Monterey. It was September, and the Santa Rosalia festival was happening. They asked me to be an angel, and to say a prayer in Italian. I was frightened and tried very hard to speak loud enough so that everyone could hear me. Then I looked up. I saw her. Santa Rosalia. She looked real—really alive to me. She seemed to be smil-

ing, and a warm feeling came over me. It was as though she knew. She knew I would be devoted to her. And I was. From then on I worked for her, honored her. I can honestly pray to her. She is truly in my heart.[20]

Vitina Spadaro found a connection to Monterey's Sicilian community through the celebration of a saint whom she was hardly aware of in the old context, but who became critical to her in the new environment, symbolizing for her everything that was good about the immigration.

Anita Ferrante recalled her mother's experience as a new immigrant from Marettimo who realized the importance of the *festa* in bringing her into the community of Sicilian women in Monterey: "They [Sicilian immigrants] were going back in their minds to the warmth of their country and bringing that feeling here. It united us. The first thing my mother did was ask to join the *festa*. That's how we were incorporated into the community; through the *festa*. That was truly how it worked. She wanted to become part of the community. And she wanted us to become part of the community too."[21]

At the same time, newer migrants helped second- and third-generation immigrants recall their identities as Sicilians. Migrants made sure that celebrations remained true to the events in Sicily. New migrants made up the bulk of the active participants in the *festa*, constantly adding vitality to the celebrations. In turn, many descendants of migrants arranged their visits to Sicilian villages to coincide with Santa Rosalia or Marettimo's important St. Joseph's *Festa* in order to experience the *festa* in the Sicilian context. The *festas* encouraged a constancy of migration in both directions that kept the process fluid and created a sense of cultural, social, economic, and political belonging to Monterey and Sicily.[22]

Transition: Post–World War II *Festa*

In the period between 1920 and Pearl Harbor, Sicilians in Monterey were not concerned about whether or not they were appreciated by the larger community of Monterey. The war changed that. The attacks on "enemy aliens" during World War II made it imperative that Sicilians not only build community among themselves but also build a bridge to the larger community of Monterey. Women used the traditional *festa* to begin the process of linkage that might head off future assaults on their community. This was evident in the changes that the Santa Rosalia *Festa* underwent after the end of World War II. Instead of coffee and homemade desserts, the entire Italian community gathered at the wharf for a gigantic barbecue. Sicilians welcomed anyone and everyone from the community of Monterey. They identified proudly as Sicilians and, at the same time, shared common ground as middle-class Americans. Santa Rosalia became a political event. "Everyone who showed up got a seat at the table. We wanted to show, 'This is who we are.' We have strong families. We work hard. We are a tight community. We are good Americans."[23]

Santa Rosalia became increasingly ostentatious and inclusive after the war years. Some of this owed simply to the increased prosperity of the Sicilian fisherpeople, who benefited enormously from the high sales of sardines that the war demanded. Only two days after the forced evacuations of "enemy aliens" from Monterey, an entire section of the *Monterey Peninsula Herald* was dedicated to the history and significance of the "booming" sardine industry.[24]

The *festa* expanded to include groups of men from various Italian organizations, such as the Sons of Italy and the Knights of Columbus, in the procession. By the end of the 1940s, a pony cart with children dressed in traditional costumes and groups of Tarantella dancers joined, along with a queen and court of the *festa*, chosen by lot from the pool of daughters of fishermen, rather than from a consensus of mothers. The women of the ICF who started the event raised money for a real stone statue. Santa Rosalia could no longer be carried, but was led through the procession on a float, which women spent weeks decorating. The simple religious event that had incorporated the culture of Monterey Sicilian fisherpeople began to look more like an American-style parade.[25]

The bishop came from San Francisco with an entourage to bless the boats en mass, rather than individually. A huge ceremonial wreath replaced the simple, small one thrown out to sea in memory of the fishermen who had died. People continued their celebrations beyond the parade with parties on the boats, which had been decorated for the occasion with garlands of flowers and Italian flags. The *Monterey Herald* ran front-page stories with full-page photographs covering the *festa*, and the city of Monterey made overtures to the ICF, wanting to run the event. Many Sicilian women in the ICF steadfastly refused their offer, fearing the loss of religious purpose. Others eventually supported the expansion.

Elite Sicilian men played a decisive role in community leadership during the years of World War II and through the experiences of exclusion. They extended their power in the community to the Santa Rosalia *Festa* and attempted to take over officially from the women of the ICF. This caused some bitterness on the part of some of the original women organizers, who felt the *festa* might lose its religious meaning and purpose in the transition. In response, women organizers Josephine Compagno, Giovanina Spadaro, and

Mary Balesteri maintained a tight control over finances, making sure all funds raised were for Santa Rosalia alone. "They really held on to that cash," recalled Marie Compagno of the efforts of the ICF women during the post-World War II years.[26] Nonetheless, the *festa* was transformed. Instead of a paean to the saint, it became a cultural extravaganza, an Italian Pride Day with less-obvious connections to religion, and more clearly a show of social as well as political strength. John Steinbeck described it as "the biggest barbecue the sardine men had ever given . . . the speeches rose to a crescendo of patriotism and good feeling beyond anything Monterey had ever heard."[27]

The ostentatious *festa* in the 1950s and 1960s signified that Monterey's Sicilians had achieved their twin goals of assimilation into both a self-identified community of fishers and an integral part of the community of Monterey. They were no longer poor fisherpeople, but people of property and civic strength who could afford to stage a real event. Some women simply dropped out at this point, citing the lack of religious piety in the Italian *festa*–turned-American parade. "It [became] a disgrace," said Jenny Russo.[28] Her friend, Angie Bruno continued, "People don't even know there is a mass. They have no respect. I told my daughter, 'Don't bother taking me. I don't want to go at all.'"[29]

St. Joseph

At this moment in time, more traditionalist Sicilians withdrew from the increasingly Americanized Santa Rosalia *Festa* and organized a spring celebration common in Marettimo: St. Joseph's *Festa*. In contrast to the politics of Santa Rosalia, the celebration of the St. Joseph's *Festa* in Monterey served not to create a bond with the city of Monterey but to maintain a link with Sicily, and particularly with the island of Marettimo. It began exactly like Santa Rosalia began, as one woman's impulse and many women's ritual. "I started this whole thing in my kitchen in 1947," said Vitina Peroni.[30] "We talked about it and we said, 'We should do St. Joseph's here [in Monterey] too,' just like we did in Marettimo," recalled Josephine Arancio.[31] The Marettimare women remembered St. Joseph's *Festa* as even more important in the context of Marettimo than the Santa Rosalia *Festa*. "In Marettimo, we didn't really celebrate Santa Rosalia that much. St. Joseph's. That was the important one."[32] Local Sicilian women bake all the special desserts consumed on the *festa* day. The event itself is carefully organized around a ritualized mass, which features the members of the holy family in a nativity scene, followed by a casual luncheon, and finally a more formal dinner/dance. It remains completely authentic—so much so that it has become a moment when friends and relatives from Marettimo plan visits to Monterey and vice-versa. Over time, the celebration has become an important marker in the calendar year for participants, who adhere to the specific rituals practiced exactly as they remember them from Marettimo.

Women emigrants from Marettimo dominated the planning and execution of St. Joseph's *Festa* to such an extent that it was difficult to find Sicilians present who originated elsewhere. Migration experiences of the Marettimares remain fresh, revitalized from a constant flow from that island. Unlike Santa Rosalia, St. Joseph's was less public, limited to a church service and banquet at the Elk's Lodge in Monterey. Though St. Joseph's included a procession down the main street of Marettimo, there were no headlines, and there was no parade in Monterey. Instead, the *festa* was focused mainly on the ritual consumption of special foods, specifically desserts and other sweets made for that occasion only. The Italian language was the dominant, if not exclusive, form of discourse at the celebration of the St. Joseph *Festa*.

According to Anna Sardinia, age sixty-three, who migrated to Monterey in 1962, St. Joseph's is the essence of identity, and Sicilian women were responsible for making it happen. "Santa Rosalia is so commercial, so American. Now they won't even raise an Italian flag. They say the mass in the Doubletree [Hotel] now, instead of the plaza. This is wrong. St. Joseph's is very different. It is small, simple. It is our faith, our belief. This is how we bring the culture to our families, our children. This is the main thing. This is the beautiful thing. For St. Joseph's, we [eight to ten Sicilian women] gather together in Bea [Bonnano's] house and make the *pignolo* and the *cubaida* [the special desserts for the *festa*]. It makes me remember the days when I was young—my grandmother. It is like being at home with all of the women together like that. The gathering—it makes you feel like you're not even here. You're there." Mrs. Sardinia's narrative demonstrates the clear cultural and religious purpose behind the *festa* and that women were its driving force. She contrasted the celebration to Santa Rosalia culturally: "[At St. Joseph's] everyone speaks our language. You feel that you really feed Jesus, Mary, and Joseph."[33]

JoAnn Mineo also reflected the poignancy of a migration that remained open-ended by using her involvement in St. Joseph's as an example of her sense of identity in two worlds. When I visited her, she was listening to the Italian-language news on television, something she is accustomed to doing. She did not attend school in the United States but is fluent in English. Still, she is more comfortable speaking Italian, specifically the Sicilian dialect. She

and her family have made countless long and short visits to her native Trapani in the years since their migration in 1970. Her son was born there. Once,
they stayed for a three-and-a-half-year sojourn. "I should own Alitalia," she
said. "We go back so much! Every year! We own land [on the island of]
Marettimo [her husband's place of origin]. It has a view of the sea. We will
build there, maybe in a year or two. We sold one house and I bought [an-
other] house. In ten years I paid it off." Yet Mrs. Mineo considers Monterey
her permanent home. "When I am there, I miss here. I miss the freedom, the
shopping, the going out, the working." For Mrs. Mineo, St. Joseph's *Festa* is
a critical connection to Sicily. Mrs. Mineo remembered the St. Joseph's *Festa* in Trapani as a citywide event: "It's not like here at all. They take the saint
through the streets. We used to hang out bedspreads from the balconies. The
people all gave money. The whole town celebrated. All the families got together. It was a big holiday. In my mother's house, we had about twenty
people. My uncle was named Joseph, like the saint, so that was a special thing.
We never made the cookies for the *festa* [as they do in Monterey]. There were
the best bakeries in Trapani! Everyone bought [from] them.[34]

Monterey's population is diverse and multicultural. It would not be possible to have the kind of citywide celebration of St. Joseph in Monterey as in
Trapani or Marettimo without a huge amount of organization and compliance on the part of the rest of the population, something that is both unlikely and unwanted by the participants. St. Joseph's is far more private an
affair for Sicilians in Monterey than for Sicilians in Sicily. "It's closer here
[in Monterey], said Mrs. Mineo. "We get together for a mass, lunch, and then
a dinner/dance. There are about 150 people who come. Everything is well
organized, small, religious. We are new and old [immigrants]. Both. It is a
time to be together." That sense of togetherness is of critical import to Mrs.
Mineo, who enthusiastically participates in the group baking and organizing
Sicilian women do in the month before the *festa* takes place. She attends
Santa Rosalia. "I go to it [Santa Rosalia], but I don't get involved. There is
too much confusion. It [Santa Rosalia] just gets bigger and bigger, with so
many booths, vendors. It's too much.[35]

Santa Rosalia, 1960s, 1970s, 1990s

However, for Sicilians who experienced the stress and dislocations during
the war years as "enemy aliens," the transformation of Santa Rosalia into an
Americanized event was a relief. They understood that they had succeeded
in accomplishing a transition for the Sicilian community from outsiders to

essential members of middle-class Monterey: "We felt at this point that we could relax. The *festa* was fun. We didn't have to prove anything to anybody. We lived and worked side by side with the people of Monterey. There was an acceptance by then [the 1960s]."[36]

The *Monterey Herald* ran full-page stories covering the festival, with another page of photographs from this decade. In dramatic contrast to the era of the 1930s, when the Santa Rosalia *Festa* was ignored by the community at large and certainly by the news media, the headline in 1952 read: "Parade is Highlight of Weekend Events Here: 20,000 Persons Watch Colorful Spectacle of Fisherman's Festival." The article was located, significantly, in the News section of the paper, right next to the editorials. The Sicilians had created a solid community that conformed to American middle-class standards and values in everything from family to patriotism. They had made their mark on the consciousness of the city by 1952. Other ethnic festivals never generated this kind of attention, indicating that the Sicilian efforts to fuse economics (fishing) with ethnic identity may have been a critical factor in establishing themselves as integral to Monterey.

According to the *Herald* article that year, 3,500 people took part in the parade itself, "in a colorful display of religious and patriotic devotion." The event was clearly meant to be both political and religious, but above all, a celebration of ethnic fishers. Photographs of smiling nuns preceding the statue of the saint in the parade were juxtaposed with Italian community leaders and local political dignitaries. There is a huge photograph of the blessing of the boats, and many shots of the bishop and religious dignitaries. Yet the article also gave a detailed description of the order of the procession, which was in marked contrast to the small religious events of the 1930s and 1940s. Political and social power, as well as cultural and spiritual solidarity, was evident in highly ritualized form:

> Leading off the parade was the civic division with city and county officials, the Monterey police and fire departments and the gaily caparisoned Monterey County Sheriff's Posse. The Festival Committee rode in a decorated purse seine skiff.
>
> Then came the military, led by a Coast Guard shore rescue unit and the crack 6th Infantry Band and a battalion of troops from Fort Ord. The Navy was represented by the Electronics Band from Treasure Island and marching units from the Postgraduate School and the Naval Auxiliary Air Station here. Two tanks made up the noisy entry from the Peninsula's National Guard outfit.[37]

The article continued to describe at some length the many drill teams, bands, drum corps, floats, and horse marching units that participated. It ended with, "And of course, the theme of the parade was emphasized by the long line of devout marchers from the Italian Catholic Federation . . . [who] carried huge rosaries fashioned out of brilliantly colored tinsel balls."[38]

Interviews and newspaper articles made clear that Sicilian men and women together led and controlled the *festa;* it remained a symbol of Sicilian community. Masculine symbols such as military marching units and bands, and representatives of local government, police, and fire-fighting units were all prominent in the celebrations that occurred in the 1950s. Women remained critical and integral actors, however, and the *festa* never lost the thread of religious purpose that continued to be the meaningful inducement for women's continued involvement, especially for newly arrived migrant women.

While Santa Rosalia represented fishing as a vital enterprise, the fishing industry was on the decline by 1952, although everyone still felt hopeful about the next season. "It wasn't like it just ended. We all thought, 'Hey, maybe next year it will be better.' So we held on. We kept going, trying to make things work," remembered Ray Lucido, who lost his cannery in these years, and was forced to drive a taxicab in order to support his family. "People got kind of quiet, depressed. We didn't want to admit things were so bad."[39]

The Santa Rosalia festival was one of the ways the Sicilian community reminded itself that it had real roots in Monterey. This was no mere labor migration that allowed for easy moves to new fishing grounds. The establishment of the *festa* by Sicilian women marked Monterey as a permanent Sicilian enclave.

Mike Maiorana recalled his own frustration at the obvious demise of the industry, but also the stubborn allegiance of Monterey fisherpeople to the Sicilian community as a permanent fixture in Monterey: "The sardines kept moving south, to San Pedro, and the fishermen in Monterey kept getting poorer and poorer. The San Pedro fishermen made money, but our families wouldn't leave. I wondered why. I asked my dad—why don't we move to San Pedro? What are we doing here? He couldn't really explain it to me, but what he said amounted to that they had a home here. They worked hard at making a community, which meant for them a physical feeling of ownership, of place. People who were rivals in Sicily came together in Monterey, even if it was only a little bit. It's remarkable that they created a community because they were always separated by village allegiances in Sicily."[40]

It was not such a mystery for Sicilian women, who were clear about their goal in community building and the permanency of the enterprise of migration. "It was the women, the wives, who wouldn't go. They had beautiful houses here, families. They weren't going to give it all up to move [to San Pedro]. So the men had to go along. They either gave up [fishing] or left their families [for months at a time] to go to San Pedro or Alaska."[41] By the middle decades of the 1960s, some families did move, mostly to the San Pedro area.

The ritual of the *festa* persisted in Monterey through the 1960s, but it was affected by the anxiety many Sicilians felt as they struggled to accept the fact that poor catches meant the imminent disappearance of sardines from the bay. Even huge tributes to Santa Rosalia would not bring back the sardines. Sicilians began to come to terms with a sense of loss, that there was an end to the abundance that had once seemed limitless. It was a moment in time when Sicilian women became entrepreneurs themselves and also encouraged entrepreneurship in their family circles, in order to maintain an economic position in Monterey beyond commercial fishing. However, they continued to identify as fishers and expressed that identity in their continued support for the Santa Rosalia *Festa*.

Entrepreneurs

Sicilian women and men participated in the new post–World War II economy of Monterey as partners in the truest sense. They became restaurateurs, grocers, contractors, retailers, and realtors. People who formerly earned their livings in commercial fishing did not abandon the enterprise altogether; they still fished for recreation and even for peripheral income, but the mainstay of family economies changed.

Anita Ferrante's family came to Monterey in 1934 from Marettimo and became prominent commercial fishermen. However, even during the heyday of sardines, Mrs. Ferrante was adamant that her parents knew enough to diversify: "They did not believe in putting all of our eggs in one basket," she said. When asked the extent to which women were involved in finances in the family, Mrs. Ferrante was clear: "You bet your life we were involved. Definitely. After my father died, especially, everything was free and clear. There were four of us, and I was in charge of investments. I took equity out of one property and put it into malls, shopping centers. I made it grow. It still supports my mother, my family."[42]

"God yes women were important. Very important. They were partners, even though we were kind of old school," said Charles Della Sala. He was a new migrant to Monterey in 1946. His wife, Rose, came from a working-class fisher family whose members worked on the fishing boats and in the canneries through the 1920s and 1930s. She was twenty-two when she met her husband at a dance at Parish Hall in San Carlos Church, shortly after he arrived in Monterey. They dated for two years, but her patience was running thin and she insisted on setting a wedding date. "I was scared," he remembered telling her, "I have no skills. I cannot work." He recalled that she assured him she would contribute. "Don't worry, she told me, I can work too. And she did. She went to work in the canneries cutting the heads off the fish. I worked as a firefighter. . . . Then we got the idea to buy a little house, a little shack, fix it up and sell it. We did that a couple of times and made a thousand dollars. We thought, hey, this is pretty good. So we kept it up. But then we thought about how much we were paying the real estate agent, so my wife got her license and she became an agent and ran the office while I worked as a firefighter. Then I became an agent and a broker too. We had five children. While I was at work, she made all the appointments, made all the decisions. We work together. We did pretty good. We own over one hundred rental units today.[43]

Vito and Pat Spadaro went into the restaurant business in 1961, "when the sardines started to go downhill." Mrs. Spadaro went to work for a title company and Mr. Spadaro tried salmon fishing for a while as a way to maintain his livelihood. "It was hard to give up [fishing]," recalled Mr. Spadaro. "When I got out of high school I started fishing and saved $10,000 in three years. It was good money in those days [1940s]." However, by 1961, "fishing was bad, bad, bad," said Mrs. Spadaro:

> We talked it over. We decided to buy a coffee shop on Alvarado Street. That was 1966. We all had to pitch in to make it work. Then urban renewal booted us out. So we bought a bar on Cannery Row, which we turned into a restaurant after a few years. That was very successful. We had some pretty rough times, but we went with the flow, the trends. At first it was formal, then not so formal. Eventually we were able to buy another restaurant on Alvarado Street. My son had a restaurant in Salinas too. Everyone worked in the restaurants. My son took a crash course in restaurant finance. My daughters all worked with us. There was a small margin in the restaurant business, but we made it because we shopped—we got the best price for produce, meat, fish. You have to watch what you buy.

Mrs. Spadaro attributes her willingness to take a risk and "energy" to her mother. "My father would go fishing in Alaska for two months or more. He gave my mother money for groceries, the household. One day, this friend of my mother's said, 'There are two houses for sale up on the hill. I think you should take a look.' So my mother looked at them, and put down payments on both of them. She had to eat pasta and bread for a month. But she said, 'You never have anything if you don't gamble.' She was the strong one; she bought real estate. She was a go-getter. That has been handed down. [Sicilian] women were strong. They sure were."

Mr. and Mrs. Spadaro sold their restaurants and retired but remain active in the Italian Catholic Federation, which continues to form the bulwark of Sicilian community life, hosting events from Lenten dinners and fund-raisers for the community to the Santa Rosalia *Festa*. At the time of this interview, Mr. Spadaro is head of the board appointed to plan Santa Rosalia for 2004.[44]

Santa Rosalia remained an important focal point throughout the transition years between 1952, when the women of the ICF ran the *festa*, and 1970, when Peter Coniglio, the mayor of Monterey and leader in the Sicilian community, revived and renamed it as *Festa Italia,* dedicated to Italians of all regions, not just Sicilians. The 1970s marked years of compromise as well as strife. The *festa* included the women of the ICF, but also involved many new members of the community who never fished or worked in canneries, and whose families were never involved in fishing.[45] It included food and craft booths, as well as bocce ball tournaments and ethnic dancing that contributed to an atmosphere of joyous celebration of Italian culture, but did not necessarily resemble the strict and authentic ritual celebrations directly related to everyday lives of the participants as fisherpeople. Still, the Sicilian fishing community turned out in force to participate. Two years later, Mayor Peter Coniglio enlisted the support of Jerome Lucido, a local banker and president of the Sons of Italy, to manage and run the reconstructed *Festa Italia.*

The changes that Mr. Coniglio made in the celebration persist into the present day. Part of that was attributable to economics. "It became really expensive to put on the *festa*. We had to insure everyone who walked in the parade, and we had to pay for everything we used. So we had to expand and include all the commercial parts," explained Vitina Spadaro.[46] Josephine Favazza restored the position of women and the ICF to the *festa* in 1990, without fanfare. In the present day it remains an event that is inclusive of the Italian community as a whole, rather than only Sicilians. Still, the women of the ICF make sure that the traditional tribute to the saint remains integral to the *festa*. Bettye Sollecito for example, maintained the traditional practice of choosing a queen to represent Santa Rosalia and, together with a committee from the ICF, of organizing the formal banquet to celebrate the coronation. The Sicilian community of Monterey continues to mark Santa Rosalia as a definitive event on the calendar. "Our worry is, will this be passed on to the younger generation? We really try to get the young families involved. Will we even have Santa Rosalia, say, twenty-five years from now?"[47]

Sicilian women invented Santa Rosalia in a political and economic context that felt hostile in the 1930s. They understood that they needed to come together as a self-defined community of fishers. After the experience of World War II, they also understood that bridges needed to be built with the rest of Monterey's populace. Sicilians showed through the public event of Santa Rosalia that they were not a political threat, but a positive social and economic entity whose presence would benefit Monterey, not endanger it.

Sicilian women took the requisite steps to do this beginning in 1937 with the public celebration of Santa Rosalia. They retreated from the public *festa* during the period of World War II, out of fear as well as out of a sense of being overwhelmed by the chaos and confusion generated by national policy toward "enemy aliens" among them. Although they resumed celebration of the *festa* after the war years, the women relinquished control over some of the *festa* events to elite males in their community who had established themselves as leaders during the crisis involving enemy aliens, even as the women maintained a strict control over funds. Santa Rosalia lost some of its religious focus in the postwar period and also gained a masculine political element. The public *festa* purposefully generated broader social appeal that proclaimed the viability, strength, and permanency of a community in the wake of threats during the war years. This new direction was supported by many women but also alienated many others, some of whom sought the old sense of pure spirituality and communal exclusivity of the St. Joseph's *Festa.*

While the significance of Santa Rosalia was increasingly public and political, the importance of St. Joseph was as critical as an ongoing link to Sicily. The celebration of St. Joseph's *Festa* in Monterey was strong evidence that Monterey has an extant Sicilian community that continues to value the connection to the homeland. Monterey's Sicilian fisherpeople, no longer dependent on fishing as a livelihood, continue to express an identity as ethnic fishers through celebrations such as St. Joseph's, which bind them culturally to their original homes in Sicily.

The two *festas* represented community and political connection to the city of Monterey. They are symbols of the complexity of acculturation as well. Santa Rosalia reminded Sicilian fisherpeople of the importance of ritual in identity, and also required Montereyans to acknowledge Sicilian fishers as critical actors in Monterey's economic and political life. St. Joseph's served as a crucial, ongoing link to homeland villages, making the concept of transnationalism a viable one.

Conclusion

Monterey, California, is a special place. It is richly diverse, both culturally and environmentally, offering scholars a unique opportunity to peer into a microcosm, to explore a complex process such as immigration in a remarkable but manageable milieu.

Once the capital of Alta California, Monterey soon became less important politically, but its economic significance grew, primarily for its role in commercial fishing, which linked California to global markets. Beginning in the mid-nineteenth century, Monterey attracted a host of immigrant fishing people looking for new resources. Chinese came looking for abalone, Russians hunted sea otters, while Portuguese hunted whales all before 1900. Japanese abalone divers and Italian and Slovenian salmon and deep-sea fishermen found a rich and diverse natural environment well into the twentieth century.

Immigrant peoples discovered that Monterey was conducive to settlement and family life as well. A mild climate and beautiful landscape attracted people used to living near the sea. Although Monterey was always populated, beginning with Native Americans and continuing with Mexicans and Spanish colonialists in the seventeenth and eighteenth centuries, the nineteenth- and twentieth-century immigrations of fishing people created a diversity of population that kept society from becoming stultified. Instead, Monterey felt both welcoming and fluid to new immigrants, with what appeared to be unlimited economic opportunity in fish species. By the first part of the century and certainly by mid-century, Monterey became not only a demographic mix, pulling diverse peoples into a new and heterogeneous mainstream, but also an urban center with ethnic enclaves, with Sicilian immigrants as the most prominent.

By 1915 the economic downturn in Sicily was growing ever more serious. Sicilians discovered that their native fish species, sardines, were available in abundance in Monterey Bay, and they too joined the migration streams of ethnic fishing peoples eagerly exploiting Monterey's plentiful resources. Then they did something different from everyone else. They drove a collective stake into Monterey that accomplished two goals: (1) redefining Sicilian immigrants as a new community of ethnic fishers, and (2) redefining Monterey as part of Sicilian cultural heritage.

I focused on the Sicilian experience in Monterey to show why and how immigration can be a deliberate process in community building and ethnic identity formation. First and foremost, I argue that women were central to every part of the process of forging and maintaining an ethnic identity; building community; and responding to all sorts of political, social, economic, and familial challenges in the course of the settlement experience beginning in 1915 and continuing into the present day. In turn, the community made room for women to act independently, even encouraged them to play central roles in everything from household finances to public displays of ethnic identity in the Santa Rosalia *Festa*.

The period between 1915 and 1970 was a time when forces came together to alter a people, Sicilian migrant fisherpeople, and a landscape, the city of Monterey, forever. Two world wars created huge demands for canned sardines to feed the military and also connected Monterey to national as well as global markets. In spite of increasingly restrictive legislation, immigrants flooded into California in this period and supplied the new sardine industry with a cheap, reliable labor force, which included women in the canneries and men on the fishing boats.

The Sicilian people who migrated to Monterey during this time came from specific, economically depressed villages on the west coast of Sicily. They made decisions to move based on a long history as migrant fisherpeople. Sicilian fisherwomen eagerly participated in this particular migration because Monterey presented a uniquely hospitable environment for them as women, as laborers, and as those experienced in the ways of fishing. From the moment of decision to migrate, Sicilian fisherwomen participated actively in the long-term processes of migration and settlement in crucial ways. Their efforts resulted in a permanently altered life for themselves and their families, and in a changed Monterey. They created an identity as Sicilian fisherpeople and kept it—even as they changed from being migrants to immigrants, from fisherpeople, in fact, to fisherpeople mostly in memory.

Sicilian women and men purposefully changed Monterey as well, from a village of native borns to an industrialized city of working-class immigrant groups. They viewed that transformation as progress. Sicilians shared an outlook that industrialization was a positive good. They saw the big fishing boats and canneries as things of beauty and were puzzled and more than a little wounded that others in Monterey considered them eyesores. Many families proudly displayed photographs of canneries and fishing boats and of themselves, friends, and family at work in the cannery, on the dock, or on the boats. Long after the end of the fishing era, Sicilians continued to look back on the years of fishing and canning as productive times, not as a destructive phase in the history of the Monterey. They shared a sense of pride in their own participation in the growth and development of the city.

Their vision was contested from the outset. In 1939 the Monterey City Council adopted a master plan to protect what it saw as the cultural integrity of the city, just as the fishing industry was entering its peak phase of development. In it, the city council recommended that "Fisherman's wharf be removed"; that "Booth's cannery . . . be removed entirely"; and that the entire downtown area was in need of "reinstatement of [its] original scenic conditions."[1] None of these recommendations became policy in 1939. Instead, the wharf area expanded; the population of working-class ethnics increased; and even more factories were built. A "working-class culture" emerged in Monterey and seemed to overwhelm the city socioeconomically.[2] The political, social, and economic forces that demanded canned and processed sardines were too formidable and easily overcame local politics. Then the huge schools of sardines disappeared.

Resource depletion was a normal part of life for Sicilian fisherpeople, as it was for fishers everywhere. Out-migration was the usual strategy for dealing with scarcity. This time, however, the Sicilians did not leave, even as the environment of the bay was polluted and depleted and the sardines disappeared. Sometime in the 1960s Sicilians faced a critical turning point as a community. Service industries that supported tourism gradually replaced fishing as the economic base for Sicilians as their families went beyond mere home ownership to investments in Monterey itself. The process of reidentification celebrated the industrialization of the past while it made Sicilian migrants aware of their concrete stake in Monterey, the city, rather than Monterey Bay. They turned their attention to the streets, the neighborhoods, the businesses that went into the creation of a city. Their ideas about development and modernization slowly transformed from factory building in support of industrialized fishing to housing development and the growth of small business such as restaurants, shops, and service-oriented enterprises. It became clear that Monterey was as valuable for its real estate and its tourist appeal as it had been for its fish. Gender had everything to do with this new economics of the Sicilian families.

Women in Sicilian families generally controlled family finances. In families of fisherpeople, women's control over important family finances was even more pronounced. Sicilian women justified purchasing real estate and diversifying the family economy in Monterey by first arguing for the importance of owning the family home and then by investing in rental properties and other small businesses as a safeguard against hard times, which they knew would come. Sicilian women successfully resisted moving to follow the fish, resulting in a large Sicilian settlement that remains as a viable community today. It became independent of fishing even as the people became increasingly identified culturally and socially with the idea of Monterey as a fishermen's town.

Women did not act in isolation. Real negotiation took place within families. Sicilian women and men chose to stay in Monterey because they had transformed it from merely a working-class, industrialized workspace. Monterey became familiar, home, a Sicilian cultural and social space. They expressed their sense of ownership in Monterey in a variety of ways, notably through the public celebration of traditional Sicilian *festas,* defining these celebrations as being as much a part of Monterey's tradition as the tradition of the villages in Sicily.

However, the transition was also marked by conflict. Class differences divided Sicilians as much as ethnicity and fishing united them. Former mayor Peter Coniglio, whose grandparents were among the earliest migrants to Monterey, remembered the period between 1957 and 1977 as one in which Sicilian working-class fisherpeople vehemently opposed the federal government's efforts to bring urban renewal and tourism, which more prosperous Sicilian business people supported just as passionately. Urban renewal meant displacement to working-class Sicilians, just as industrialized fishing had displaced poor Mexican workers in Monterey in the 1920s, 1930s, and 1940s. The city was "torn up for sixteen years" and people were "bitter, angry." People were reimbursed for their property, but they did not want to leave. "They were a people who had to see the water from their windows—nothing could convince them there was any other way to live."[3]

The downtown and wharf areas were the only places directly affected by urban renewal. Most of the other working-class neighborhoods remained unchanged. Still, working-class Sicilian fisherpeople fought government policies they thought threatened their cultural space, as they readjusted to the new reality that Monterey would no longer allow them to live by fishing. Sicilians became politically active. In 1960 Frank Bruno led a recall of public officials in an attempt to forestall urban renewal. In 1963 a hastily organized group of local developers led by Joseph Fratessa tried to circumvent plans for development by forming their own development agency. "I remember the whole town was upset," recalled Lucy Ventimiglia Gruwell. "It was all politics. The government wanted to take away everything that made Monterey a fishing town, a seashore town. They ended up taking away all the old residences, all the homes, all the old buildings. They tore down the Dollar store. That was a landmark. They made everything that was homes into offices, big buildings. We were all against it."[4]

Sicilian middle-class women meanwhile led families on a new economic path, cementing the transition by continuing to create social and cultural ways of consolidating their stake in the city of Monterey itself. They vigorously expanded the public celebrations of Sicilian *festa*. They continued to invest in many forms of real estate, especially in small businesses and commercial and residential real estate. They increased the number and participation in organizations whose sole purpose was a nostalgic celebration of Sicilian cultural identity as fisherpeople. All of this attracted the attention of the local media reinforcing the idea of Monterey as deeply influenced by Sicilian fisherpeople—socially, culturally, and historically.

The urban renewal controversy was resolved in 1977 under Mayor Peter Coniglio, who helped direct rebuilding effort towards the Monterey Conference Center, which became the focal point for a redefined city whose economic base was clearly built on tourism, not fishing. From 1977 to the present day, Monterey Sicilians supported the direction of re-creating Monterey as a tourist center, but one based on nostalgic historical memory. The restoration of the old adobes, the Custom House Plaza, and the reinvention of Cannery Row are all parts of that historic reinvention. Sicilian migrants and their descendants consider their ethnic contribution to the cultural landscape of Monterey preeminent, and work actively to incorporate their experience in Monterey as a critical part of the historical landscape.

The goals of Sicilian migrants, women and men, gradually shifted from fishing to the development of Monterey itself. Sicilians transformed their efforts from factory building to building restaurants, from creating working-class neighborhoods to re-creating city landscapes to commemorate a cultural ideal and ethnic memory. In so doing they attached themselves more closely to their roots, visiting Sicily far more frequently in recent years than their parents and grandparents were able to or interested in doing. As a result, the connections between Sicilians in Monterey and the villages remain surprisingly strong. Intermarriage with native Sicilians and Sicilians native to Monterey, while not commonplace, is also not uncommon.

Much has been written about the population of migrant Italians, both from the north and from the south. Yet, most of this literature focuses on agricultural or industrial workers. Italian fisherpeople share a common culture with other Italians of their region and class, but they also passionately identify as fisherpeople and, as such, demonstrate behaviors and values quite different from their compatriots. One of the most critical differences has to do with gender roles and perceptions of place for women. Attitudes and practices with regard to gender became critical in the experience of immigration and shaped their experiences in profound ways.

The story of Sicilian migration to and from Monterey incorporates the experiences of Sicilian fisherpeople into the literature on immigration, particularly on Italian immigration, and also fits into a growing scholarship on migration that focuses on individuals and families without denying structural patterns and world systems as important factors in migration processes. This new scholarship stresses the importance of women and women's roles in migration without artificially separating gender analysis from ethnicity, race, or class. Gender, ethnicity, and class are fused, in individuals, in families, and in communities.

Moreover, as the newest scholarship on migration makes clear, immigrants generally change their destination sites every bit as much as the destination sites transform the immigrants. This Monterey case study demonstrated that the migration of Sicilians shaped the growth, development, and conceptualization of Monterey as an ethnic industrial working-class fishing town. The consequence in the present day is an immediate sense of cultural connection to fishing villages in Sicily and the movement of peoples to and from both sides of the ocean.

Migration is not an event but a process. This case study of Sicilians in Monterey, California, is a relatively recent phenomenon and still in progress, which allowed for the extensive use of oral history as a method of analysis. Although limited in some ways, the oral accounts collected here from ordinary people proved to be a rich, complex, and valuable resource that gave me critical insight into the study of migration.

The experience of Sicilian migrants to (and from) Monterey, California, from the period just before 1920 and through the present day, demonstrated a pattern of chain migration based on a fusion of occupation, region, and kinship. The Sicilians' construction of identity as fisherpeople and kinfolk, from specific villages in Sicily to a specific environment in Monterey, created this migration chain.

As the Sicilian community matured with the growth of the fishing industry from 1920 until its demise in 1948, women made a crucial difference at a critical moment in the process of migration. They made sure that families invested in the environment itself. They not only bought homes, but they also bought rental property and even small businesses. They laid the groundwork for continued settlement rather than continued migration. They formed themselves into ritualized prayer groups and craft groups that overcame divisions among themselves based on *campanilismo* and kinship and connected with one another into the larger whole of a Sicilian ethnic community. They then led the way in connecting this Sicilian community to the larger society of Monterey by including American elements in the public celebrations of the saints. When the sardines disappeared, and some families moved on to find them, many more had already grown deep roots in their community through the decisions and behavior of women. It became unthinkable to resume the historical pattern of migration.

Men played a different role in the migration and settlement process at that particular moment in time—the period of World War II in the wake of the forced evacuations of aliens from the California coast, particularly from Monterey. Elite Sicilian men took a public, proactive role in defining the Sicilian community to the wider society as economically essential, law-abiding, and loyal to the American government. Their insistent, and public, definition of American citizens influenced community conceptions of identity so that American citizenship was fused with ethnicity, not set in opposition to it. After the war, they began to play an active and influential role in local politics and also became actively involved in the religious celebration of the *festa*, which they helped transform into an event that was essentially an American political celebration.

By the 1970s, in the wake of the Civil Rights Movement and an increasing level of ethnic awareness in the United States, Sicilians began to think differently about cultural roots. There was a resurgence of both scholarly and popular interest in ethnicity. Oral histories, community studies, and festivals celebrating ethnic heritage were all evidence of growing interest in ethnicity throughout the country, particularly in California. Sicilians in Monterey began recording their own migration stories, revisiting their home villages, learning Italian, or just brushing up on the Sicilian dialect. The travel industry boomed, making it possible to spend vacations in Sicily or send offspring to stay with kin for the summer. This had a powerful consequence. Without affecting the permanency of the Monterey settlement, it became possible for an increase in a new fluidity of migration to occur between Sicilian villages and Monterey. Migration had always continued, but the travel industry and the renewal of interest in ethnic "roots" made visits and migrations commonplace, casual, even frequent.

The once inhospitable economy of Sicily improved as a result of tourism and travel. Families who remembered great poverty found themselves property owners in resort towns. Families used capital from Monterey to build restaurants and hotels in San Vito Lo Capo, Isola Della Femina, and Marettimo. Teenagers found summer jobs in both locations. Young adults found jobs too, and marriage partners, and began raising families in both settings. Sicilian families in Monterey continue to incorporate new migrants. Migrants bring a sense of transition with them, a feeling of belonging to two worlds at once. This sense is carried through to kin and community so that a feeling of internationalism is present even among Sicilians who never venture out of Monterey.

I meant to give women in the Sicilian community in Monterey their rightful place as migrants and community builders in this analysis. I spent years listening to their stories and experiences, as well as those of their husbands and children. I concluded that they and their mothers and grandmothers were not only integral to migration, but in large part responsible for its outcome. Women continue to play important roles as decision makers as the process of migration and settlement continues. They share a role with fisherwomen in other cultures, times, and places. They are central, not marginal, in their families and communities.

Sicilian women saw opportunities for themselves in the burgeoning new economy of Monterey. Many found husbands among the fishermen, paid work in the canneries, an opportunity to exercise increased social freedom, and a place to create home and community in Monterey. They cooperated in initiating a migration process that, because of their advocacy, almost immediately changed from temporary fishing sojourns to family migration and permanent settlement. They defined home in a profound way for their families, indeed for their community as a whole.

Notes

Introduction

1. Interview with Elizabeth "Liz" Grammatico, August 25, 2004.

2. Federal Manuscript Census, Monterey County, 1920; Walton, *Storied Land,* 192.

3. Walton, *Storied Land,* chapters 3 and 4.

4. McEvoy, *Fisherman's Problem;* Walton, *Storied Land;* Friday, *Organizing Asian-American Labor.*

5. Ibid. See also Lydon, *Chinese Gold;* Yamada, *Japanese of the Monterey Peninsula.*

6. Fitzgerald, "Hovden Cannery"; Cutino, *Monterey;* Mangelsdorf, *History of Steinbeck's Cannery Row.*

7. Rosenberg, "History of Industries"; Monterey Fisherman's Historical Association, Oral Histories, 1995; Cutino, *Monterey.*

8. Walton, *Storied Land;* Nokunas, *Politics of Public Memory.*

9. Castanada, "Spanish-Mexican Women"; Walton, *Storied Land;* Haas, *Conquests and Historical Identities;* Monroy, *Thrown among Strangers.*

10. Nokunas, *Politics of Public Memory.*

11. Walton, "Cannery Row," 243–97.

12. Hall, Leloudis, Korstad, Murphy, Jones, and Daly, eds., *Like a Family,* 172–73, 308, 310–11.

13. Reeder, "Conflict across the Atlantic," 371–91; Reeder, "When the Men Left Sutera," 45–67.

14. Quotation from McGoodwin, *Crisis in the World's Fisheries,* 30.

15. The relatively new field of marine anthropology (post-World War II), which specializes in studying fishing people and cultures, is summarized in McGoodwin, *Crisis in the World's Fisheries,* chapter 2.

16. Binkley, *Set Adrift: Fishing Families.* See also work by Nadel-Klein and Davis, eds., *To Work and to Weep,* and Marechal, ed., *Women in Artisanal Fisheries.*

17. Gabaccia and Iacovetta, eds., *Women, Gender, and Transnational Lives;* Glick-Schiller, Basch, and Blanc-Szanton, eds., "Towards a Transnational Perspective"; Hondagneu-Sotelo, ed., *Gender and U.S. Immigration;* Portes and Rumbaut, eds., *Ethnicities.*

18. Ruiz, *Cannery Women, Cannery Lives;* Zavella, *Women's Work and Chicano Families.*

19. See Haas's analysis of the construction of ethnic identity in *Conquests and Historical Identities,* and Monroy, *Thrown among Strangers.*

20. Ruiz, *Cannery Women, Cannery Lives;* Zavella, *Women's Work and Chicano Families.*

Chapter 1: Sicilian Women, Fishing Lives, and Migration Strategies

1. Federal Manuscript Census, Monterey County, 1880.

2. Ibid.

3. See Walton, *Storied Land;* Haas, *Conquests and Historical Identities;* Monroy, *Thrown Among Strangers.*

4. Federal Manuscript Census, Monterey County, 1880.

5. Ibid.

6. Ibid.

7. Walton, *Storied Land,* chapter 4; Fink, *Monterey County,* 132; Nokunas, *Politics of Public Memory;* Conway, *Monterey.*

8. Federal Manuscript Census, Monterey County, 1900.

9. Federal Manuscript Census, Monterey County, 1910.

10. Yamada, *Japanese of the Monterey Peninsula.*

11. Monterey County Tax Assessment, 1914.

12. Oral Histories, Monterey Fishermen's Historical Association, 1995.

13. Johnston, *Old Monterey County,* 96.

14. Federal Manuscript Census, Monterey County, 1920.

15. Interview with Mike Maiorana, June 2, 1993.

16. Interview with Frances Archdeacon, November 3, 1992.

17. Monterey City Directories, El Monte, Calif.: R. L. Polk & Co., 1905, 1907, 1926, 1930, 1933, 1937, 1939, 1941, 1947, 1949, 1951, 1953–1960; Walton, *Storied Land;* Cutino, *Monterey;* Hemp, *Cannery Row;* Manglesdorf, *History of Steinbeck's Cannery Row;* Reinstadt, *Where Have All the Sardines Gone?;* Conway, *Monterey.*

18. Federal Manuscript Census, Monterey County, 1920.

19. U.S. Census Records.

20. Monterey County Tax Assessor Records, 1940–1961.

21. Ibid.

22. McGoodwin, *Crisis in the World's Fisheries,* 3.

23. Ibid., 65.

24. See Binkley, *Set Adrift: Fishing Families;* Brettell, *We Have Already Cried;* Bourne, *View from Front Street;* Cole, *Women of the Praia;* Sant'Ana Diegues, ed., *Tradition and Social Change;* Ellis, *Fisher Folk;* Feinberg, ed., *Seafaring in Contemporary Pacific Islands;* Hviding, *Guardians of Marovo Lagoon;* Kennedy, *People of the Bays and Headlands;* Nadel-Klein and Davis, eds., *To Work and to Weep;* Mauk, *Colony That Rose from the Sea;* Miller, *Salt in the Blood;* Smith, ed., *Those Who Live from the Sea;* Spoehr, *Maritime Adaptions; Women in Fishing Communities: Guidelines, A Special Target Group of Developments Projects,* Food and Agriculture Organization of the United States, 1993; Taylor, *Documenting Maritime Folk Life,* American Folk Life Center; Zaya, *Two Japanese Maritime Communities;* Maril, *Texas Shrimpers,* 90.

25. McGoodwin, *Crisis in the World's Fisheries,* 25, 38–39.

26. Maril, *Texas Shrimpers,* 90.

27. Vaccaro, "Marettimo and Monterey," 15.

28. Interview with Theresa Sollazzo, February 9, 1996.

29. Interview with Mike Mellusi, June 6, 1997.

30. Interview with Anita Ferrante, April 2, 1997.

31. Cole, *Women of the Praia,* 63; See also Binkley, *Set Adrift: Fishing Families;* Nadel-Klein and Davis, eds., *To Work and to Weep;* Smith, ed., *Those Who Live from the Sea.*

32. Interview with Antoinette Corbello (pseudonym), January 10, 1999.

33. Interview with Maria Mineo, October 3, 1994.

34. Interview with Hope Cardinalli, October 5, 1995.

35. Interview with Theresa Sollazzo, October 5, 1995.

36. See studies by Hamilton, 1992–2001, on environment and social change in the North Atlantic arc, particularly Hamilton, Lyster, and Otterstad, "Social Change, Ecology, and Climate"; Hamilton and Haedrich, "Fishing Communities of the North Atlantic Arc"; Hamilton and Otterstad, "Demographic Change," 16–22; Hamilton, Rasmussen, Flanders, and Seyfrit, "Outmigration and Gender Balance," 89–97. See also Andersen, ed., *North Atlantic Maritime Cultures;* Fisher, ed., *Man and the Maritime Environment;* Harris, *Lament for an Ocean; Demographic Change in Coastal Fishing Communities and Its Implications for the C Fisheries,* U.S. Food and Agriculture Department; McGoodwin, *Cultures of Fishing Communities;* Poggie and Pollnac, eds., *Small-Scale Fishery Development.*

37. Gatewood and McKay, "Job Satisfaction," 12. Quotation from McGoodwin, *Crisis in the World's Fisheries,* 23.

38. Vaccaro, "Marettimo and Monterey," 5.

39. Ibid.

40. Gabaccia and Iacovetta, eds., *Women, Gender, and Transnational Lives;* Caroli et al. *Italian Immigrant Woman;* Cohen, *Workshop to Office;* DiLeonardo, *Varieties of Ethnic Experience;* Gabaccia, *From Sicily to Elizabeth Street;* Gabaccia, *From the Other Side;* Friedman-Kasaba, *Memories of Migration;* Bocia-Mule, *Authentic Ethnicities;* Iacovetta, *Such Hardworking People;* Iacovetta, *Nation of Immigrants;* Yans-McLaughlin, *Family and Community.*

41. Gabaccia and Iacovetta, *Women, Gender, and Transnational Lives,* 11.

42. Castles and Miller, *Age of Migration;* Koser and Lutz, *New Migration in Europe;* Kofman, "Female Birds of Passage," 269–99.

43. Bodnar, *Transplanted;* Simon and Brettel, eds., *International Migration;* Foner, *New Immigrants in New York.*

44. Foner, *New Immigrants in New York,* 244.

45. Portes, "Immigration Theory," 816.

46. Bodnar, *Transplanted,* 84.

47. Ibid.

48. Grasmuck and Pessar, *Between Two Islands,* 15. See also chapter 5.

49. Ibid., 15.

50. See Ewen, *Immigrant Women,* 33–35.

51. Interview with Ray Lucido, November 10, 1996.

52. Ibid.

53. Vecoli, "Contadini in Chicago," 404–17; Yans-McLaughlin, *Family and Community*.

54. Ibid. See also Cinel, *National Integration*; Caroli et al. *Italian Immigrant Woman*; Gabaccia, *From Sicily to Elizabeth Street*.

55. Foerster, *Italian Immigration*.

56. Interview with Giovanna "Jenny" Lucido Costanza, September 2, 1994.

57. Interview with Salvatore Ferrante, courtesy of Rosalie Ferrante, August 10, 1996.

58. Interview with Vitina Spadaro, February 19, 1997.

59. Ewen, *Immigrant Women*, 55–56.

60. Interview with Joseph Favazza, March 10, 1997.

61. Interview with Joseph Favazza, September 30, 1995.

62. Interview with Nancy Mangiapane, October 26, 1997.

63. Collins, *Pioneer Italian Fishermen*.

64. Cinel, *From Italy to San Francisco*.

65. Interview with Maria Mineo, August 12, 1994.

66. Interview with Maria Mineo, September 2, 1994.

67. Interview with Anita Ferrante, April 2, 1997.

68. Basch, Glick-Schiller, and Blanc-Szanton, *Nations Unbound*, 6.

69. Interview with Linda Saccomanno (pseudonym), September 9, 1994.

70. Interview with Natale Pizzamente (pseudonym), Marettimo, Sicily, June 15, 1998.

71. Interview with Ursula Anaclero (pseudonym), San Vito Lo Capo, Sicily, June 8, 1998.

72. Interview with Marielena Spadaro, September 16, 1996.

73. Interview with Catherine Caliri (pseudonym), June 2, 1994.

74. Interview with Rose Ann Aliotti, July 7, 1997.

75. See Walton, *Storied Land*, and Davis, "Sardine Oil on Troubled Water."

76. Caroli, et. al., *Italian Immigrant Woman*; Cohen, *Workshop to Office*; DiLeonardo, *Varieties of Ethnic Experience*; Gabaccia, *From Sicily to Elizabeth Street*; Gabaccia, *From the Other Side*; Yans-McLaughlin, *Family and Community*.

77. See Massey, *Return to Aztlan*; Sassen, *Losing Control?*; Portes and Rumbaut, *Immigrant America*; Lin Lim, Smith, and Dissanayake, eds., *Transnational Asia Pacific*; Foner, ed., *New Immigrants in New York*; Hondagneu-Sotelo, ed., *Gender and U.S. Immigration*.

78. See Anthias and Lazardis, *Gender and Migration*, chapters 5 and 7; Castles and Miller, *Age of Migration*, 125 and chapter 11.

79. Anthias and Lazardis, *Gender and Migration*, 114.

80. Ibid., 118–21.

81. Hollifield, "Politics of International Migration," 143.

Chapter 2: Work and Identity

1. Cole, *Women of the Praia*, chapter 4.

2. There is considerable and continuing scholarly debate about the extent to which assimilation takes place, and why. Though it is no longer considered a simple linear process determined by generation, there is agreement that it is the desirable outcome

generally, both on the part of the immigrants and the host culture. This general agreement focuses on immigrants, not migrant laborers.

3. Yans-McLaughlin, *Family and Community;* Vecoli, "Contadini in Chicago," 404–17; Iacovetta, *Such Hardworking People;* Gabaccia, *From Sicily to Elizabeth Street;* Gabaccia, *Militants and Migrants;* Gabaccia, *From the Other Side;* Cohen, *Making a New Deal.*

4. Walton, "Cannery Row," 244; See also Walton, *Storied Land,* chapter 5, and Rosenberg, "History of Industries."

5. Davis, "Sardine Oil on Troubled Water," chapter 2; See Ruiz, *Cannery Women, Cannery Lives,* chapter 2.

6. Interview with Mary Soto, September 9, 1999.

7. Interview with Lenore Pelligrino (pseudonym), July 6, 1994.

8. Interview with Juanita Segovia, September 20, 1998.

9. Davis, "Sardine Oil on Troubled Water," chapter 2.

10. Monterey City Directories, 1924–1951.

11. Davis, "Sardine Oil on Troubled Water," 62; Fitzgerald, "Hovden Cannery"; Cutino, *Monterey;* Mangelsdorf, *History of Steinbeck's Cannery Row.*

12. Interview with Annette Balestreri, February 23, 1991.

13. Monterey Bay Aquarium Historic Documentation Program, 2002–2004. See also Davis, "Sardine Oil On Troubled Water," 63–66.

14. Interview with Angie Bruno, January 8, 1991.

15. Interview with Eleanor Fugetta, July 16, 1991.

16. Walton, *Storied Land;* interview with Susan Shillinglaw, director of the Steinbeck Institute, May 22, 2004.

17. Sutherland, "Earnings and Hours," 22.

18. Interview with Annette Balestreri, July 15, 1991.

19. Interview with Nancy Mangiapane, July 12, 1991.

20. Interview with Thelma Francioni, July 22, 1991.

21. Interview with Rose Salimento, June 17, 1991.

22. Interview with Yvonne Russo Humbracht, August 5, 1991.

23. Interview with Eleanor Fugetta, September 2, 1991.

24. Interview with Dolly Ursino and Eleanor Fugetta, September 2, 1991.

25. Interview with Nancy Mangiapane, September 11, 1991.

26. Davis, "Sardine Oil on Troubled Water," chapter 2; Hovden Company Records; Walton, *Storied Land,* chapter 5.

27. Interview with Esperanza Ventimiglia Ernandes, September 10, 1991.

28. Interview with Phyllis Taormina, December 17, 1991.

29. Interview with Catherine Cardinale, August 19, 1992.

30. Interview with Lucy Ventimiglia Gruwell, September 19, 2001.

31. Interview with Angie Bruno, June 14, 1991.

32. Interview with Lucy Ventimiglia Gruwell, September 19, 2003.

33. Ibid.

34. Interview with John "Bricky" Crivello, June 5, 1996.

35. Letter to AFL Council, March 20, 1939.

36. Davis, "Sardine Oil on Troubled Water," chapter 2.

37. Letter from Western Director, AFL, to Sec. of Seine-Line Fisherman's Union, Monterey, July 1, 1939.

38. For an analysis of Italian women's activism, see Gabaccia, *Militants and Migrants;* Glenna Matthews, *Silicon Valley,* chapter 2. For radical labor activism among sardine cannery works, see Davis, "Sardine Oil on Troubled Water," chapter 2.

39. Interview with Angie Bruno, March 20, 1996.

40. Interview with Eleanor Fugetta, October 12, 1995.

41. Interview with Nancy Mangiapane, May 13, 1995.

42. Interview with Joann Silva, September 20, 1998.

43. Interview with Sarah Sousa and Mary Silva, January 7, 1991.

44. Interview with Thelma Francioni, February 2, 1991. Narrators used "Spanish" rather than "Mexican" to identify Hispanic ethnicity.

45. Interview with Esther Campoy, January 9, 1991.

46. Interview with Dorothy Wheeler, January 6, 1990.

47. Interview with Eleanor and George Salimento, October 12, 1991.

48. Ruiz, *Cannery Women, Cannery Lives,* 82.

49. Davis, "Sardine Oil on Troubled Water," chapter 2.

50. Interview with Catherine Cardinale, October 24, 1995.

51. Interview with Eleanor Fugetta, July 24, 1992.

52. Interview with Catherine Cardinale, November 13, 1993.

53. Interview with Phyllis Taormina, March 1, 1991.

54. Interview with Esperanza Ventimiglia Ernandes, May 1990.

55. Ibid.

56. Interview with Yvonne Russo Humbracht, January 12, 1991.

57. Gabbacia, *Militants and Migrants.*

58. Interview with Phyllis Taormina, November 18, 1993.

59. Interview with Esperanza Ventimiglia Ernandes, December 2, 2000.

60. Ibid.

61. Interview with Mike Maiorana, November 12, 1996.

62. Interview with Geno Marazzini (pseudonym), March 2, 1995.

63. Interview with Arturo Pagnini (pseudonym), May 6, 1995.

64. Interview with Nancy Magini, July 10, 1991.

65. Interview with Mary Aiello, August 6, 1992.

66. Interview with Rose Cutino, October 17, 1994.

67. Interview with Nancy Mangiapane, August 7, 1991.

68. Interview with Catherine Cardinale, March 7, 1998.

69. Interview with Angie Bruno, October 7, 1994.

70. Interview with Dolly Ursino, March 15, 1998.

71. Interview with Frances Archdeacon, June 4, 1991.

72. Interview with Rose Salimento, June 4, 1991.

73. Interview with Anna Grillo (pseudonym), October 12, 1998.

74. Interview with Rose Cutino, July 10, 1993.

75. Interview with Mary Anne Alliotti, Rose Marie Cutino Topper, and Rosalie Ferrante, June 2, 1996.

76. Ibid.

77. Interview with Rose Salimento, April 6, 1991.

78. Interview with Rose Marie Cutino Topper, October 22, 1998.

79. DiLeonardo, *Varieties of Ethnic Experience;* Matthews, *Silicon Valley.*

80. Ruiz, *Cannery Women, Cannery Lives;* Zavella, *Women's Work and Chicano Families.*

81. Ruiz, *Cannery Women, Cannery Lives;* Zavella, *Women's Work and Chicano Families.*

82. Davis, "Sardine Oil on Troubled Water," chapter 2.

83. Interview with Pat Spadaro, March 10, 1997.

84. Interview with Joseph and Josephine Favazza, September 1, 1994.

85. Monterey County Tax Assessor Records, 1924.

86. Polk's Monterey Directory, 1951. Property ownership was indicated by a special marking—a circle within a circle next to the name of the person listed.

87. Monterey County Tax Assessor, Records, 1910–1960.

88. Ibid.

89. Ibid.

90. Interview with Nancy Tarantino Iliffe, September 26, 1996.

91. For a more extensive analysis of the advent of purse seiners, see Davis, "Sardine Oil on Troubled Water."

92. Interview with Peter Cutino, November 2, 1994.

93. Interview with Peter Cutino, November 2, 1994; Interview with Mike Maiorana, November 7, 1994.

94. Interview with Peter Cutino, November 2, 1994.

95. Interview with Catherine Cardinale, October 25, 1995.

Chapter 3: Family, Conflict, Community

1. County of Monterey Office of the Recorder Clerk, Marriage License Records, 1906–1979.

2. Ibid.

3. Bell, *Fate and Honor;* Schneider and Schneider, *Culture and Political Economy,* 207.

4. McGoodwin, *Crisis in the World's Fisheries.*

5. Cinel, *From Italy to San Francisco,* 221.

6. Interview with Anita Ferrante, October 22, 1996.

7. Interview with Rosalie Ferrante, September 4, 1995.

8. Interview with Katy Reina (pseudonym), July 18, 1996.

9. Interview with Maxine Palluzzi (pseudonym), November 2, 1996.

10. Gabaccia, *From the Other Side,* 78–79.

11. Hall, Leloudis, Korstad, Murphy, Jones, and Daly, eds., *Like a Family,* 172–73, 308, 310–11.

12. Interview with Maria Mineo, September 27, 1996.

13. Interview with Maria Mineo, September 27, 1996. I attended several different rosary groups from 1990 to 1997. These conclusions are based on my personal observations.

14. Interview with Nancy Mangiapane, August 19, 1991.

15. Interview with Esperanza Ventimiglia Ernandes, July 17, 1991.

16. Interview with Yvonne Russo Humbracht, July 17, 1991.

17. Interview with Eleanor Fugettta, August 4, 1992.

18. Interview with Nancy Mangiapane, August 4, 1992.

19. Interview with Rosalie Ferrante, April 16, 1993.

20. Interview with Rose Marie Cutino Topper, January 6, 1994.

21. Interview with Jack and Janet Russo, August 26, 2004.

22. Interview with Catherine Cardinale, July 22, 1992, and Jack and Janet Russo, August 26, 2004.

23. Interview with Lucy Ventimiglia Gruwell, September 22, 2001.

24. Interview with Rosalie Ferrante, November 1, 1996.

25. Cutino, *Monterey.*

26. Interview with Peter Coniglio, July 8, 1997.

27. Interview with Phyllis Taormina, October 7, 1994.

28. Interview with Frank and Francesca Nuovo, October 13, 1994.

29. Interview with Mike Maiorana, July 12, 1997.

30. Interview with Erasmo Peraino (pseudonym), July 2, 2003.

31. Ibid.

32. See DiLeonardo, *Varieties of Ethnic Experience;* Matthews, *Silicon Valley;* Gabbacia, *Militants and Migrants;* Yans-McLaughlin, *Family and Community.*

33. Interview with Rose Enea, August 27, 1996.

34. Interview with Mary Ferrante Coniglio, October 10, 1996.

35. Ruiz, *Cannery Women, Cannery Lives;* Zavella, *Women's Work and Chicano Families.*

36. Interview with Mary Buffo, May 10, 1995.

37. Interview with Rose Marie Cutino Topper, January 6, 1994.

38. Interview with Lucy Ventimiglia Gruwell, August 27, 2004.

39. Interview with Lorraine Fazzini (pseudonym), February 7, 1996.

40. Interview with Josephine Vultaggio (pseudonym), August 19, 1995.

41. Ibid.

42. Interview with Dorothy Vienna Amato (pseudonym), November 13, 1996.

43. Interview with Lillian Castrucci Sanchez (pseudonym), June 2, 1996.

44. Ibid.

45. Ibid.

46. Interview with Mary Longueria, September 20, 1998.

47. Interview with Juanita Segovia, September 20, 1998.

48. Interview with Emily Rodriquez, September 20, 1998.

49. Interview with Rose Davi, August 9, 1994.

50. Interview with Joe Sollecito, September 4, 1996.

Chapter 4: Good Americans

1. See Moch, *Moving Europeans;* Lucassen and Lucassen, *Migration, Migration History, History;* Massey, ed., *Becoming American, American Becoming.*

2. See Brubaker, ed., *Immigration;* Brubaker, *Citizenship and Nationhood;* Hollifield,

"Immigration"; Hollifield, "Politics of International Migration," 162–73; Schuck, *Citizens, Strangers and In-Betweens.*

3. See McGoodwin, *Crisis in the World's Fisheries;* Spoehr, *Maritime Adaptions;* Maril, *Texas Shrimpers.*

4. Interview with Mary Brucia Darling, November 16, 1997.

5. Ibid.

6. Walton, *Storied Land,* 200–213.

7. Gabaccia, *Militants and Migrants.*

8. Interview with Peter Coniglio, October 24, 1995.

9. Interview with Joe Sollecito, October 27, 1995.

10. Interview with Albert Mangiapane, May 5, 1998.

11. Interview with Peter Cutino, May 14, 1998.

12. DiLeonardo, *Varieties of Ethnic Experience;* Cinel, *From Italy to San Francisco.*

13. Lothrup, "Shadow on the Land," 189–211.

14. Ibid., 194–97.

15. Ibid., 194.

16. Ibid., 200.

17. Interview with Peter Cutino, May 14, 1998.

18. Lothrup, "Shadow on the Land," 206.

19. Yamada, *Japanese of the Monterey Peninsula.*

20. Interview with Rose Aiello Cutino, April 16, 1998.

21. Interview with Peter Cutino, May 14, 1998.

22. *Monterey Peninsula Herald,* December 15, 1941.

23. Ibid., December 9, 1941.

24. Ibid., December 14, 1941.

25. Ibid., December 15, 1941.

26. Ibid., December 10, 1941.

27. U.S. Congress, *Report of the Select Committee Investigating National Defense Migration,* 2.

28. *Monterey Peninsula Herald,* December 20, 1941.

29. "Impact of Air Attack," Stanford Research Institute; Hixon, ed., *American Experience;* Rosenberg, *Date Which Will Live;* Starr, *Embattled Dreams.*

30. *Monterey Peninsula Herald,* February 20, 1941.

31. Rosenberg, *Date Which Will Live,* chapter 3.

32. Interview with Nancy Mangiapane, October 12, 1995.

33. Interview with Gaetano Rossetti (pseudonym), November 2, 1995.

34. Interview with Gaspar Aliotti courtesy of Rosalie Ferrante, May 2, 1998.

35. Interview with Rose Davi, December 18, 1995.

36. Interview with Mary Anne Aliotti, February 3, 1997.

37. *Monterey Peninsula Herald,* December 17, 1941.

38. Ibid., December 16, 1941.

39. See Lipsitz, *Possessive Investment in Whiteness.*

40. Interview with Giuseppe Spadaro, September 22, 1995.

41. Rosenberg, *Date Which Will Live,* chapter 8.

42. Lopez, *White by Law,* 42.

43. Ibid., 45–47. See also Guglielmo and Salerno, eds., *Are Italians White?*

44. Smith, *Civic Ideals,* 3; Guglielmo and Salerno, eds., *Are Italians White?*

45. Lopez, *White by Law;* Jacobson, *Whiteness of a Different Color;* Lipsitz, *Possessive Investment in Whiteness.*

46. Kerber, *No Constitutional Right.*

47. Jacobson, *Whiteness of a Different Color;* Guglielmo and Salerno, eds., *Are Italians White?;* Guglielmo, *White on Arrival.*

48. *Monterey Peninsula Herald,* December 15, 1941.

49. Ibid., December 13, 1941.

50. Ibid., February 7, 1942.

51. Ibid.

52. Ibid., February 17, 1941.

53. Interview with Betty Lucido, May 11, 1998.

54. *Monterey Peninsula Herald,* February 17, 1941.

55. Interview with Vincent Bruno, May 20, 1998.

56. *Monterey Peninsula Herald,* February 2, 1942.

57. Ibid., February 7, 1942.

58. Interview with John Mercurio, April 20, 1998.

59. Interview with Rose Aiello Cutino, August 18, 1996.

60. Interview with Joe Favazza, February 12, 1997.

61. *Monterey County Herald,* February 17, 1942.

62. Interview with Rosalie Ferrante, May 17, 1998.

63. Interview with Giovanna "Jenny" Costanza, August 7, 1996.

64. Interview with Catherine Lococo, July 10, 1995.

65. Interview with Mike Maiorana, September 2, 1998.

66. Interview with Peter Cutino, April 8, 1998.

67. Interview with Mary Anne Aliotti, April 16, 1998.

68. She was referring to the 1907 Naturalization Act and the Cable Act of 1922, which disallowed citizenship granted automatically to spouses of naturalized citizens. Symposium, Monterey Conference Center, 1994.

69. Interview with Catherine Lococo, July 10, 1995.

70. *Monterey Peninsula Herald,* December 12, 1941.

71. Ibid.

72. Ibid., December 17, 1941.

73. Interview with Jack Russo, November 10, 1995.

74. Interview with Mary Brucia Darling, November 16, 1997.

75. Interview with Peter Coniglio, December 8, 1998.

76. Interview with Jenny Russo, September 6, 1995.

77. *Monterey County Herald,* December 1941–1945.

78. Rosenberg, *Date Which Will Live,* chapter 8; Yamada, *Japanese of the Monterey Peninsula.*

79. Interview with Mike Maiorana, August 1, 1995.

80. *Monterey Peninsula Herald,* February 11, 1942.

81. Ibid., December 13, 1941.

82. Ibid., February 11, 1942.

83. Ibid., December 12, 1941.

84. Ibid., February 11, 1942.

85. Ibid., December 13, 1941.

86. Ibid., February 21, 1942.

87. Ibid.

88. Ibid., February 7, 1942.

89. Symposium, Monterey Conference Center, 1994.

90. Interview with Vita Crivello Davi, August 17, 1994.

91. Forum on Italian Internment, Monterey Conference Center, September 14, 1994.

92. Interview with Mary Anne Aliotti, August 10, 1994.

93. Interview with Josephine Favazza, August 15, 1994.

94. Interview with Joseph Favazza, September 19, 1994.

95. Interview with Catherine Lococo, July 10, 1995.

96. Interview with Ray Lucido, August 4, 1997.

97. Interview with Rose Marie Cutino Topper, August 22, 1994.

98. Interview with Mike Maiorana, August 1, 1995.

99. Interview with Ray Lucido, August 4, 1997.

100. Interview with Joe Cardinale, September 10, 1994.

101. Interview with Jenny Costanza, August 12, 1996.

102. Rosenberg, *Date Which Will Live,* 147–54.

103. Fox, *Unknown Internment;* DiStasi, ed., *Una Storia Segreta.*

104. DiStasi, *Una Storia Segreta,* 6.

105. Ibid., 21.

106. Ibid.

107. Fox, *Unknown Internment,* chapter 4.

Chapter 5: Women on Parade

1. DiLeonardo, *Varieties of Ethnic Experience,* chapter 6.

2. Ibid., 215.

3. Binkley, *Set Adrift: Fishing Families;* Brettell, *We Have Already Cried;* Cole, *Women of the Praia;* Diegues, ed., *Tradition and Social Change;* Nadel-Klein and Davis, eds., *To Work and to Weep;* Smith, ed., *Those Who Live from the Sea.*

4. Personal observations in rosary groups, 1990–98.

5. Binkley, *Set Adrift: Fishing Families;* Brettell, *We Have Already Cried;* Cole, *Women of the Praia;* Diegues, ed., *Tradition and Social Change;* Nadel-Klein and Davis, eds., *To Work and to Weep;* Smith, ed., *Those Who Live from the Sea.*

6. See chapter 3.

7. Vecoli, "Contadini in Chicago," 404–17; Orsi, *Madonna of 115th Street.*

8. Interview with Jenny Russo and Angie Bruno, November 10, 1994.

9. Interview with Theresa Canepa, February 24, 1998.

10. Italian Heritage Society Historical Publication, September 8–9, 1979.

11. Interview with Jenny Russo and Angie Bruno, November 10, 1994.

12. *What's Doing,* 1937.

13. D'Avee, "Monterey and the Canned Sardine."

14. Interview with Jenny Russo and Angie Bruno, July 6, 1995. Bonnie Gartshore, Santa Rosalia festival articles, *Monterey Peninsula Herald,* 1990–96.

15. Interview with Catherine Lococo, September 10, 1994.

16. Interview with Theresa Canepa, February 24, 1998.

17. Interview with Josephine Giamona Weber, July 2, 1994.

18. Interview with Catherine Cardinale, October 5, 1994.

19. Interview with Jenny Russo and Angie Bruno, November 10, 1994.

20. Interview with Vitina Spadaro, September 1, 1995.

21. Interview with Anita Ferrante, September 5, 1995.

22. Interviews conducted at Santa Rosalia *Festa* and St. Joseph's *Festa,* Monterey, 1996–98.

23. Interview with Rosalie Ferrante, September 12, 1996.

24. *Monterey Peninsula Herald,* February 27, 1942.

25. Ibid., September editions from 1940 to 1944.

26. Interview with Marie Compagno, August 30, 2004.

27. See Walton, "Cannery Row," 266; Steinbeck, *Cannery Row,* 24–25.

28. Interview with Jenny Russo and Angie Bruno, November 10, 1994.

29. Ibid.

30. Interview with Vitina Peroni.

31. Interview with Josephine Arancio, July 16, 1996.

32. Interview with Anna Sardinia, March 10, 2005.

33. Ibid.

34. Interview with JoAnn Mineo, March 8, 2005.

35. Ibid.

36. Interview with Josephine Arancio, July 16, 1996.

37. *Monterey Peninsula Herald,* September 9, 1952.

38. Ibid.

39. Interview with Ray Lucido, August 10, 1997.

40. Interview with Mike Maiorana, August 3, 1995.

41. Interview with Catherine Cardinale, May 2, 1999.

42. Interview with Anita Ferrante, May 16, 2003.

43. Interview with Charles Della Sala, May 14, 2004.

44. Interview with Vito and Pat Spadaro, May 17, 2004.

45. Interview with Peter Coniglio, August 10, 2004.

46. Interview with Vitina Spadaro, September 1, 2004.

47. Interview with Pat and Vito Spadaro, May 17, 2004.

Conclusion

1. Master Plan of the City of Monterey, 1939, 17.

2. Walton, "Cannery Row."

3. Interview with former mayor Peter Coniglio, April 22, 1997.

4. Interview with Lucy Ventimiglia Gruwell, September 19, 2003.

Bibliography

Primary Sources

MANUSCRIPT CENSUSES

City of Pittsburg, Calif., 1903 Census.
Monterey County, Calif., Tax Assessor Records, 1910–1960.
U.S. Bureau of the Census. Federal Manuscript Census, Monterey County, Calif., 1880, 1900, 1910, 1915, 1920.

THESES, DISSERTATIONS, PAPERS, AND
UNPUBLISHED MANUSCRIPTS

Castanada, Antonia. "Presadarias y Popladoras: Spanish-Mexican Women in Frontier Monterey, Alta California, 1770–1821." Ph.D. diss., University of California, Berkeley, 1990.
Colletto, Salvatore. "Autobiography." N.p., n.d.
Davis, Kate. "Sardine Oil on Troubled Water: The Boom and Bust of California's Sardine Industry, 1905–1955." N.p., 2002.
Enea, Robert, ed. *Sicilian Family Genealogies, 1880–1960.* N.p., n.d.
Fitzgerald, Donald. "The History and Significance of the Hovden Cannery, Cannery Row, Monterey, California, 1914–1973." Monterey, Calif.: Monterey Bay Aquarium Foundation, 1979.
Italian Heritage Society Historical Publication, 1979.
Rosenburg, Earl H. "A History of the Fishing and Canning Industries in Monterey, California." Master's thesis, University of Nevada, 1961.
Vaccaro, Leonarda. "Marettimo and Monterey: Two Communities in Comparison." Master's thesis, University of Palermo, 1995.

GOVERNMENT DOCUMENTS

Collection of American Federation of Labor Documents. Monterey History and Art Museum, Special Collections.

"Demographic Change in Coastal Fishing Communities and Its Implications for the California Fisheries, 2000." U.S. Food and Agriculture Department.

"Documenting Maritime Folk Life." U.S. Government Printing Office, Folk Life Center, 1994.

"Earnings and Hours in the Pacific Coast Fish Canneries." Arthur T. Sutherland. Bulletin of the Women's Bureau, No. 186. Department of Labor, Washington D.C., n.d.

"Impact of Air Attack in World War II, Selected Data for Civil Defense Planning." Stanford Research Institute, Stanford, Calif., n.d.

Master Plan of the City of Monterey, Calif., 1939.

Monterey City Directories. El Monte, Calif.: R. L. Polk & Co., 1905, 1907, 1926, 1930, 1933, 1937, 1939, 1941, 1947, 1949, 1951, 1953–1960, 1962–1966, 1968–1982, 1985–1987.

Monterey County Records of Marriage Licences, Monterey, Calif., 1906–1979.

Personal Justice Denied: Report of the Commission on Wartime Relocation and Internment of Civilians. Washington, D.C., and San Francisco: Civil Liberties Public Education Fund. Seattle and London: University of Washington Press, 1982 and 1983.

Report of the Select Committee Investigating National Defense Migration. U.S. Congress. House. 77th Cong., 2d sess., H.R. 1911.

"Women in Fishing Communities: Guidelines, a Special Target Group of Development Projects." Food and Agriculture Organization of the United States, 1993.

INTERVIEWS

Aiello, Diana. Interview by author. Monterey, Calif., 1995.

Aiello, Giovanni and Rose. Interview by author. Monterey, Calif., 1997.

Aiello, Mary and Neno. Interview by author. Monterey, Calif., 1997.

Aiello Family. Interview by author. Monterey, Calif., 1995.

Aliotti, Gaspar and Maryanne. Interview by author. Monterey, Calif., 1994–96.

Aliotti, Josephine. Interview by author. Monterey, Calif., 1994.

Aliotti, Marie. Interview by author. Monterey, Calif., 1995.

Aliotti, Rose Ann. Interview by author. Monterey, Calif., 1997.

Amato, Dorothy Vienna (pseudonym). Interview by author. Monterey, Calif., 1996.

Ambrosio, K. Interview by author. Monterey, Calif., 1998.

Arancio, Joseph and Josephine. Interview by author. Monterey, Calif., 1993–94.

Arancio, Ursula. Interview by author. Monterey, Calif., 1995–98.

Archdeacon, Frances. Interview by author. Monterey, Calif., 1990–94.

Balbo Family. Interview by author. Monterey, Calif., 1995.

Balesteri Family. Interview by author. Monterey, Calif., 1994.

Balestreri, Annette and Dominic. Interview by author. Monterey, Calif., 1990–98.

Balestreri, Crocifissa. Interview by author. Monterey, Calif., 1998–99.

Battaglia, Nancy. Interview by author. Monterey, Calif., 1998.

Bommarito Family. Interview by author. Monterey, Calif., 1995.

Bruno, Angie. Interview by author. Monterey, Calif., 1991–97.

Bruno, Mrs. Gus. Interview by author. Monterey, Calif., 1994.

Bruno Family. Interview by author. Monterey, Calif., 1993–94.

Buffo Family. Interview by author. Monterey, Calif., 1996.

Campoy, Esther. Interview by author. Monterey, Calif., 1990–91.

Candelario, Emily. Interview by author. Monterey, Calif., 1998.

Canepa, Theresa. Interview by author. Monterey, Calif., 1998.

Caniglia, Lena. Interview by author. Monterey, Calif., 1996.

Cardinale, Catherine and Joe. Interview by author. Monterey, Calif., 1994–2004.

Cardinale Family. Interview by author. Monterey, Calif., 1992–98.

Cardinalli, Hope and John. Interview by author. Monterey, Calif., 1998.

Cariglio, Marielena Spadaro. Interview by author. Monterey, Calif., 1995–98.

Cefalu Family. Interview by author. Monterey, Calif., 1995.

Colletto, Sal. Interview by author. Monterey, Calif., 1995–96.

Compagno, Catherine. Interview by author. Monterey, Calif., 1997.

Compagno, Katherine. Interview by author. Monterey, Calif., 1998.

Compagno, Marie. Interview by author. Monterey, Calif., 2004.

Coniglio, Mary Ferrante. Interview by author. Monterey, Calif., 1992–95.

Coniglio, Peter. Interview by author. Monterey, Calif., 1995–2004.

Costanza, Giovanna "Jenny" and Rocco. Interview by author. Monterey, Calif., 1994–99.

Criscuolo Family. Interview by author. Monterey, Calif., 1995.

Crivello, John. Interview by author. Monterey, Calif., 1996.

Crivello, John "Bricky," business agent for the Fishermen's Union from 1937 to 1998. Interview by author. Monterey, Calif., 1996.

Crivello, Josephine. Interview by author. Monterey, Calif., 1995.

Crivello, Paula. Interview by author. Monterey, Calif., 1998.

Crivello Family. Interview by author. Monterey, Calif., 1994–99.

Cutino, Peter and Louise. Interview by author. Monterey, Calif., 1995–2004.

Cutino, Rose. Interview by author. Monterey, Calif., 1994–96.

Darling, Mary Brucia. Interview by author. Monterey, Calif., 1996–97.

Davi, Jeff. Interview by author. Monterey, Calif., 1996.

Davi, Rose. Interview by author. Monterey, Calif., 1994.

Davi, Vita Crivello. Interview by author. Monterey, Calif., 1996–97.

Davi Family. Interview by author. Monterey, Calif., 1994–96.

Della Sala, Charles. Interview by author. Monterey, Calif., 1994–2004.

DiMaggio, Dario and Maria. Interview by author. Monterey, Calif., 1998.

Dimaggio, Neno and Mary. Interview by author. Monterey, Calif., 1996.

Dimaggio, S. Interview by author. Monterey, Calif., 1996.

Enea, Domenica. Interview by author. Monterey, Calif., 1996.

Enea, Robert. Interview by author. Monterey, Calif., 1992–99.

Enea Family. Interview by author. Monterey, Calif., 1994.

Ernandes, Esperanza Ventimiglia. Interview by author. Monterey, Calif., 1993–94.

Favazza, Joseph and Josephine. Interview by author. Monterey, Calif., 1992–2004.

Favolora Family. Interview by author. Monterey, Calif., 1996.

Ferrante, Anita Maiorana. Interview by author. Monterey, Calif., 1996–2004.

Ferrante, Rosalie. Interview by author. Monterey, Calif., 1992–2004.

Ferrante, Sal. Interview by author. Monterey, Calif., 1996.

Ferrante Family. Interview by author. Monterey, Calif., 1994.

Francioni, Thelma. Interview by author. Seaside, Calif., 1990–92.

Fugetta, Dolly. Interview by author. Monterey, Calif., 1990–92.

Fugetta, Eleanor. Interview by author. Monterey, Calif., 1990–94.

Gartshore, Bonnie. Interview by author. Monterey, Calif., 1995.

Giamona Family. Interview by author. Monterey, Calif., 1995.

Grammatico, Elizabeth "Liz". Interview by author. Monterey, Calif., 2003–04.

Gruwell, Lucy Ventimiglia. Interview by author. Monterey, Calif., 2003–04.

Guerra, Pina. Interview by author. Marettimo, Sicily, 1998.

Humbracht, Yvonne Russo. Interview by author. Monterey, Calif., 1990–92.

Iliffe, Nancy Tarantino. Interview by author. Monterey, Calif., 1996.

Lococo, Catherine. Interview by author. Monterey, Calif., 1995–98.

Longueria, Mary. Interview by author. Monterey, Calif., 1998.

Lucido, Betty. Interview by author. Monterey, Calif., 1992.

Lucido, Francesca. Interview by author. Monterey, Calif., 1995.

Lucido, Katherine (Kay). Interview by author. Monterey, Calif., 1998.

Lucido, Mary. Interview by author. Monterey, Calif., 1998.

Lucido, Ray "Spats". Interview by author. Monterey, Calif., 1992–98.

Lucido, Salvatore. Interview by author. Monterey, Calif., 1994–98.

Macaluso, Phyllis and George. Interview by author. Monterey, Calif., 1990 and 1994.

Maiorana, Mike. Interview by author. Monterey, Calif., 1993–99.

Mangiapane, Nancy and Albert. Interview by author. Monterey, Calif., 1990–2004.

Marcuso, Faye. Interview by author. Monterey, Calif., 1994–96.

Marotta, Mike. Interview by author. Monterey, Calif., 1996.

Melicia Family. Interview by author. Monterey, Calif., 1998.

Mello, Anna. Interview by author. Monterey, Calif., 1994.

Mercurio, John. Interview by author. Monterey, Calif., 1998.

Mercurio Family. Interview by author. Monterey, Calif., 1995.

Mineo, JoAnn. Interview by author. Monterey, Calif., 2005.

Mineo, Maria. Interview by author. Monterey, Calif., 1992–98

Noto, Carmelita. Interview by author. Monterey, Calif., 1998.

Nuovo, Frank and Francesca. Interview by author. Monterey, Calif., 1994–96.

Nuovo Family. Interview by author. Monterey, Calif., 1998.

Palma, Orsola. Interview by author. San Vito Lo Capo, Sicily, 1998.

Peraino, Erasmo (pseudonym). Interview by author. Monterey, Calif., 2003.

Peroni, Vitina. Interview by author. Monterey, Calif., 1998.

Pugh, Rose. Interview by author. Monterey, Calif., 1996.

Randazzo Family. Interview by author. Monterey, Calif., 1994.

Riso Family. Interview by author. Monterey, Calif., 1996.

Rodriquez, Emily. Interview by author. Monterey, Calif., 1998.

Rossetti, Gaetano (pseudonym). Interview by author. Monterey, Calif., 1995.

Russo, Jack and Janet. Interview by author. Monterey, Calif., 2004.

Russo, Jenny. Interview by author. Monterey, Calif., 1995.

Russo, Phyllis. Interview by author. Monterey, Calif., 1990–94.

Russo, Virginia. Interview by author. Monterey, Calif., 1995.

Salimento, Rose and George. Interview by author. Monterey, Calif., 1990–2000.

Salmeri, Mary Berry. Interview by author. Monterey, Calif., 1993.

Sanchez, Lillian Castrucci (pseudonym). Interview by author. Monterey, Calif., 1996.

Sardina, Anna. Interview by author. Monterey, Calif., 2005.

Segovia, Juanita. Interview by author. Monterey, Calif., 1997–98.

Shillinglaw, Susan, director of the Steinbeck Institute. Interview by author. Monterey, Calif., 2004.

Silva, Mary. Interview by author. Monterey, Calif., 1990–94.

Sino Family. Interview by author. Monterey, Calif., 1992.

Sollazzo, Theresa. Interview by author. Del Ray Oaks and Monterey, Calif., 1992–2000.

Sollecito, Bettye and Joe. Interview by author. Monterey, Calif., 1998.

Soto, Mary. Interview by author. Monterey, Calif., 1999.

Sousa, Sara. Interview by author. Seaside, Calif., 1990–2000.

Spadaro, Joseph and Vitina. Interview by author. Monterey, Calif., 1997–2004.

Spadaro, Vito and Pat. Interview by author. Monterey, Calif., 1996–2004.

Taormina, Phyllis. Interview by author. Seaside, Calif., 1993–96.

Taormina Family. Interview by author. Monterey, Calif., 1994.

Tarantino, Jeannette Davi. Interview by author. Monterey, Calif., 1994–2000.

Tarantino Family. Interview by author. Monterey, Calif., 1994.

Tardio, Pauline. Interview by author. Monterey, Calif., 1996.

Tardio, S. Interview by author. Monterey, Calif., 1996.

Topper, Rose Marie Cutino. Interview by author. Monterey, Calif., 1993–2004.

Triana, Domenica. Interview by author. Monterey, Calif., 1994.

Ventimiglia, Horace. Interview by author. Monterey, Calif., 1997.

Ventimiglia, Phyllis. Interview by author. Monterey, Calif., 1995–99.

Wheeler, Dorothy. Interview by author. Monterey, Calif., 1990–2004.

Secondary Sources

Andersen, Raoul, ed. *North Atlantic Maritime Cultures: Anthropolical Essays on Changing Adaptations.* New York: Mouton, 1979.

Anthias, Floya, and Gabriella Lazardis. *Gender and Migration in Southern Europe: Women on the Move.* New York: Oxford, 2000.

Arlacci, Pino. *Mafia, Peasants and Great Estates: Society in Traditional Calabria.* Cambridge, U.K.: Cambridge University Press, 1980.

Bancroft, Hubert Howe. *The Native Races of the Pacific States of North America.* New York: Appleton, 1874.

Barth, Gunther. *Bitter Strength: A History of the Chinese in the United States, 1850–1870.* Cambridge, Mass.: Harvard University Press, 1964.

Basch, L. G., N. Glick-Schiller, and C. Blanc-Szanton. *Nations Unbound: Transnational Projects, Post-Colonial Predicaments, and Deterrorized Nation-States.* Langhorne, Pa.: Gordon and Breach, 1994.

Bean, Walter E. *California: An Interpretive History.* New York: McGraw-Hill, 1973.

Bell, Rudolph. *Fate and Honor, Family and Village: Demographic and Cultural Change in Italy since 1800.* Chicago: University of Chicago Press, 1979.

Belliotti, Raymond A. *Seeking Identity: Individualism versus Community in an Ethnic Context.* Lawrence: University of Kansas Press, 1995.

Binkley, Marian. *Set Adrift: Fishing Families.* Toronto: University of Toronto Press, 2002.

Bodnar, John. *The Transplanted: A History of Immigrants in Urban America.* Bloomington: Indiana University Press, 1985.

———. *Worker's World: Kinship, Community, and Protest in an Industrial Society, 1900–1940.* Baltimore: Johns Hopkins University Press, 1982.

Boscia-Mule, Patricia. *Authentic Ethnicities: The Intersection of Ideology, Gender, Power, and Class in the Italian-American Experience.* Westport, Conn. and London: Greenwood Press, 1999.

Bourne, Russell. *View from Front Street: Travels through New England's Historic Fishing Communities.* New York: W. W. Norton Co., 1989.

Brettell, Caroline B. *Men Who Migrate, Women Who Wait: Population and History in a Portuguese Parish.* Princeton, N.J.: Princeton University Press, 1986.

———. *We Have Already Cried Many Tears: The Stories of Three Portuguese Migrant Women.* Prospect Heights, Ill.: Waveland Press, 1995.

Brettell, Caroline B., and James F. Hollifield. *Migration Theory: Talking across Disciplines.* New York: Routledge, 2000.

Brubaker, Rogers, ed. *Citizenship and Nationhood in France and Germany.* Cambridge, Mass.: Harvard University Press, 1992.

———. *Immigration and the Politics of Citizenship in North America.* Lanham, Md.: University Press of America, 1989.

Cardella, Lara. *Good Girls Don't Wear Trousers.* New York: Arcade Publishing, 1994.

Caroli, Betty B., et al. *The Italian Immigrant Woman in North America.* Toronto: Multicultural History Society of Ontario, 1978.

Castles, Stephen, and Mark Miller. *The Age of Migration: International Population Movements in the Modern World.* New York: Guilford Press, 1998.

Cinel, Dino. *From Italy to San Francisco: The Immigrant Experience.* Stanford, Calif.: Stanford University Press. 1974.

———. *The National Integration of Italian Return Migration, 1870–1929.* Cambridge, U.K.: University of Cambridge Press, 1991.

Cohen, Lisbeth. *Making a New Deal: Industrial Workers in Chicago, 1919–1939.* Cambridge, England: Cambridge University Press, 1990.

Cohen, Miriam. *Workshop to Office: Two Generations of Italian Women in New York City, 1900–1950.* Ithaca, N.Y.: Cornell University Press, 1992.

Cole, Sally Cooper. *Women of the Praia: Work and Lives in a Portuguese Coastal Community.* Princeton, N.J.: Princeton University Press, 1991.

Collins, Katherine "Tina" Davi. *Pioneer Italian Fishermen of Martinez "Nostri Pescatori."* Martinez, Calif.: the author, 1997.

Conway, J. D. *Monterey: Presidio, Pueblo, Port.* Charleston, S.C.: Arcadia Publishing, 2003.

Cornelisen, Ann. *Women of the Shadows: A Study of the Wives and Others of Southern Italy.* New York: Penguin, 1976.

Cornford, Daniel. *Working People of California.* Berkeley: University of California Press, 1995.

Corradini, Anna Maria. *Meteres: il mito del matriarcato in Sicilia.* Enna, Sicily: Papiro, 1997.

Coser, Rose Laub, Laura S. Anker, and Andrew J. Perrin. *Women of Courage: Jewish and Italian Immigrant Women in New York.* Westport, Conn.: Greenwood Press, 1999.

Cross, Ira B. *A History of the Labor Movement in California.* Berkeley: University of California Press, 1935.

Cutino, Peter J. *Monterey—A View from Garlic Hill.* Pacific Grove, Calif.: Boxwood Press, 1995.

DeJong, Gordon F., Kerry Richter, and Pimonpan Isarabhakdi. "Gender, Values, and Intentions to Move in Rural Thailand." *International Migration Review* 30, 3 (1996): 748–70.

Diegues, Antoino Carlos Sant'Ana, ed. *Tradition and Social Change in the Coastal Communities of Brazil: A Reader of Maritime Anthropology.* São Paolo: University of São Paolo Press, 1992.

DiLeonardo, Micaela. *The Varieties of Ethnic Experience: Kinship, Class and Gender among California Italian-Americans.* Ithaca, N.Y.: Cornell University Press, 1994.

DiStasi, Leonard. *Una Storia Segreta: When Italian Americans Were "Enemy Aliens."* Berkeley, Calif.: Heyday Books, 1994.

Ellis, Carol. *Fisher Folk: Two Communities on Chesapeake Bay.* Lexington: University of Kentucky, 1986.

Evans, Sara M. *Born for Liberty: A History of Women in America.* New York: The Free Press, 1989.

Ewen, Elizabeth. *Immigrant Women in the Land of Dollars: Life and Culture on the Lower East Side, 1890–1925.* New York: Monthly Review Press, 1985.

Feinberg, Richard, ed. *Seafaring in Contemporary Pacific Islands: Studies in Continuity and Change.* De Kalb: Northern Illinois University Press, 1995.

Filangeri, Carlotta. *Femmine di Sicilia: societa e cultura nella storia della Sicilia.* Siracusa, Sicily: Ediprint, 1995.

Fink, Augusta. *Monterey County: The Dynamic Story of Its Past.* Santa Cruz, Calif.: Western Tanager Press, 1982.

Fisher, Stephen, ed. *Man and the Maritime Environment.* Exeter, U.K.: University of Exeter Press, 1994.

Foerster, R. F. *The Italian Immigration of Our Times.* Cambridge, Mass.: Harvard University Press, 1919.

Foner, Nancy. "The Immigrant Family: Cultural Legacies and Cultural Changes." *International Migration Review* 31, 4 (1997): 961–75.

———. *New Immigrants in New York.* New York: Columbia University Press, 1996.

Fox, Stephen. *The Unknown Internment: An Oral History of the Relocation of Italian Americans during World War II.* Boston: Twayne Publishers, 1990.

Friday, Chris. *Organizing Asian-American Labor: The Pacific Coast Canned Salmon Industry, 1870–1942.* Philadelphia: Temple University Press, 1992.

Friedman-Kasaba, Kathie. *Memories of Migration: Gender, Ethnicity, and Work in the Lives of Jewish and Italian Women in New York, 1870–1924.* Albany: State University of New York Press, 1996.

Gabaccia, Donna Rae. *From Sicily to Elizabeth Street: Housing and Change among Italian Immigrants.* Albany: State University of New York Press, 1984.

———. *From the Other Side: Women, Gender, and Immigrant Life in the U.S., 1820–1990.* Bloomington: Indiana University Press, 1994.

———. *Militants and Migrants: Rural Sicilians Become Migrant Workers.* New Brunswick, N.J.: Rutgers University Press, 1988.

———. *Seeking Common Ground: Multidisciplinary Studies of Immigrant Women in the United States.* Westport, Conn.: Praeger, 1992.

Gabaccia, Donna Rae, and Franca Iacovetta, eds. *Women, Gender, and Transnational Lives: Italian Workers of the World.* Toronto: University of Toronto Press, 2002.

Galtung, Johan. *Members of Two Worlds: A Development Study of Three Villages in Western Sicily.* New York: Columbia University Press, 1971.

Gambino, Richard. *Blood of My Blood: The Dilemma of the Italian-American.* Garden City, N.Y.: Doubleday, 1974.

Gatewood, John B., and Bonnie J. McKay. "Job Satisfaction and the Culture of Fishing: A Comparison of Six New Jersey Fisheries." *Maritime Anthropological Studies* 1, 2 (1989): 12.

Gjerde, Jon. *From Peasants to Farmers: The Migration from Balestrald, Norway to the Upper Middle West.* New York: Cambridge University Press, 1985.

Glick-Schiller, Nina, Linda Basch, and Cristine Blanc-Szanton, eds. "Towards a Transnational Perspective on Migration, Race, Class, Ethnicity, and Nationalism Reconsidered." *Annals of the New York Academy of Sciences.* Vol. 645. New York, 1992.

Grasmuck, Sherri, and Patricia Pessar. *Between Two Islands: Dominican International Migration.* Berkeley: University of California Press, 1991.

Green, Nancy L. *Ready-to-Wear and Ready-to-Work: A Century of Industry and Immigrants in the Women's Garment Trade, Paris and New York.* Durham: Duke University Press, 1997.

Grele, Ronald. "Listen to Their Voices: Two Case Studies in the Interpretation of Oral History Interviews." *Oral History Review* 7 (spring 1979): 33–42.

Guglielmo, Jennifer, and Salvatore Salerno, eds. *Are Italians White? How Race Is Made in America.* New York: Routledge, 2003.

Guglielmo, Thomas. *White on Arrival: Italians, Race, Color, and Power in Chicago, 1890–1945.* Oxford, England: Oxford University Press, 2003.

Gumina, Deanna Paoli. *The Italians of San Francisco, 1850–1930.* New York: Center for Migration Studies, 1978.

Haas, Lisbeth. *Conquests and Historical Identities in California, 1769–1936.* Berkeley: University of California Press, 1995.

Hall, Jacquelyn Dowd, James Leloudis, Robert Korstad, Mary Murphy, LuAnn Jones, and Christopher B. Daly, eds. *Like A Family: The Making of a Southern Cotton Mill World.* Chapel Hill: University of North Carolina Press, 1987.

Hamilton, L. C., and R. L. Haedrich. "Ecological and Population Changes in Fishing Communities of the North Atlantic Arc." *Polar Research* 18, 2 (1999): 383, 388.

Hamilton, L. C., P. Lyster, and O. Otterstad. "Social Change, Ecology, and Climate in 20th Century Greenland." *Climatic Change* 47 (1999): 193, 211.

Hamilton, L. C., and O. Otterstad. "Demographic Change and Fisheries Dependence in the Northern Atlantic." *Human Ecology Review* 75, 1 (1998): 16–22.

Hamilton, L. C., R. O. Rasmussen, N. E. Flanders, and S. L. Seyfrit. "Outmigration and Gender Balance in Greenland." *Arctic Anthropology* 33, 1 (1999): 89–97.

Handlin, Oscar. *The Uprooted.* 2d ed. Boston: Little, Brown, 1973.

Hareven, Tamara. *Family Time and Industrial Time: The Relationship Between Family and Work in a New England Industrial Community.* Cambridge, U.K.: Cambridge University Press, 1982.

Harris, Michael. *Lament for an Ocean: The Collapse of the Atlantic Cod Fishery: A True Crime Story.* Toronto: McClelland and Stewart, 1998.

Hatton, Timothy, and Jeffrey G. Williamson. *The Age of Mass Migration: Causes and Economic Impact.* New York: Oxford University Press, 1998.

Heizer, Robert F., and Alan J. Almquist. *The Other Californians: Prejudice and Discrimination under Spain, Mexico, and the United States to 1920.* Berkeley: University of California Press, 1972.

Hemp, Michael. *Cannery Row: A History of Old Ocean Avenue.* Pacific Grove, Calif.: The History Company, 1986.

Hilowitz, Jane. *Economic Development and Social Change in Sicily.* Cambridge, U.K.: Schenkman Publ. Co., 1976.

Hixon, Walter L., ed. *The American Experience in World War II.* New York: Routledge, 2003.

Hoerder, Dirk, ed. *Labor Migration in the Atlantic Economies: The European and North American Working Classes in the Period of Industrialization.* Westport, Conn.: Greenwood Press, 1985.

———. "Segmented Macrosystems and Networking Individuals: The Balancing Functions of Migration Processes." In *Migration, Migration History, History,* eds. Jan Lucassen and Leo Lucassen. Bern: Peter Lang, 1997.

Hollifield, James F. "Immigration and the Politics of Rights." In *Migration and the Welfare State in Contemporary Europe,* eds. Michael Bommes and Andrew Geddes. London: Routledge, 2000.

———. "The Politics of International Migration." In *Migration Theory: Talking across Disciplines,* eds. Caroline B. Brettell and James F. Hollifield. New York: Routledge, 2000, 143.

Hondagneu-Sotelo, Pierrette, ed. *Gender and U.S. Immigration: Contemporary Trends.* Berkeley: University of California Press, 1999.

Hviding, Edvard. *Guardians of Marovo Lagoon: Practice, Place, and Politics in Maritime Melanesia.* Honolulu: University of Hawaii Press, 1996.

Iacovetta, Franca. *A Nation of Immigrants: Women, Workers, and Communities in Canadian History, 1840s-1960s.* Toronto: University of Toronto Press, 1998.

———. *Such Hardworking People: Italian Immigrants in Postwar Toronto.* Montreal: Mc-Gill-Queen's University Press, 1992.

Jacobson, Matthew Frye. *Whiteness of a Different Color: European Immigrants and the Alchemy of Race.* Cambridge, Mass.: Harvard University Press, 1998.

Jacoby, Tamar, ed. *Reinventing the Melting Pot: The New Immigrants and What It Means to Be American.* New York: Basic Books, 2004.

Johnston, Robert B. *Old Monterey County.* Monterey, Calif.: the author, 1970.

Kennedy, John Charles. *People of the Bays and Headlands: Anthropological History and the Fate of Communities in the Unknown Labrador.* Toronto: University of Toronto Press, 1995.

Kerber, Linda K. *No Constitutional Right to Be Ladies: Women and the Obligations of Citizenship.* New York: Hill and Wang, 1998.

Kessner, Thomas. *The Golden Door.* New York: Oxford University Press, 1977.

Kettner, James. *The Development of American Citizenship 1608–1870.* Chapel Hill: University of North Carolina Press, 1978.

Klein, Jane Nadel, and Dona Lee Davis, eds. "To Work and To Weep: Women in Fishing Economies." *Social and Economic Papers 18.* Institute of Social and Economic Research, University of Essex, U.K., 1988.

Kofman, Eleonore. "Female Birds of Passage a Decade Later: Gender and Immigration in the European Union." *International Migration Review* 33 (summer 1999): 269–99.

Koser, Khalid, and Helma Lutz. *The New Migration in Europe: Social Constructions and Social Realities.* New York: St. Martin's Press, 1998.

LeMay, Michael C. *U.S. Immigration: A Reference Handbook.* Santa Barbara, Calif.: ABC Clio, 2004.

Lim, Shirley Geok-Lin, Larry E. Smith, and Wimal Dissanayake, eds. *Transnational Asia Pacific: Gender, Culture, and the Public Sphere.* Urbana: University of Illinois Press, 1999.

Lipsitz, George. *The Possessive Investment in Whiteness: How White People Profit from Identity Politics.* Philadelphia: Temple University Press, 1998.

Lopez, Ian F. Haney. *White by Law: The Legal Construction of Race.* New York and London: New York University Press, 1996.

Lopreato, Joseph. *Italian-Americans.* New York: Random House, 1970.

Lothrup, Gloria Ricci. "A Shadow on the Land: The Impact of Fascism on Los Angeles Italians." In *Fulfilling the Promise of California: An Anthology of Essays on the Italian American Experience in California,* Gloria Ricci Lothrup, ed. Spokane, Wash.: California Italian American Task Force and The Arthur H. Clark Co., 2000.

Lucassen, Jan, and Leo Lucassen. *Migration, Migration History, History: Old Paradigms and New Perspectives.* Bern: Peter Lang, 1997.

Lydon, Sandy. *Chinese Gold: The Chinese in the Monterey Bay Region.* Capitola, Calif.: Capitola Book Co., 1985.

Manglesdorf, Tom. *A History of Steinbeck's Cannery Row.* Santa Cruz, Calif.: Western Tanager Press, 1986.

Marechal, Catherine, ed. *Women in Artisanal Fisheries.* IDAF Newsletter (June). Cotonou, Benin: FAO, 1988.

Maril, Robert Lee. *Texas Shrimpers: Community, Capitalism, and the Sea.* College Station: Texas A & M University Press, 1983.

Massey, Douglas S. *Return to Aztlan: The Social Processes of International Migration from Western Mexico.* Berkeley: University of California Press, 1987.

———, ed. *Becoming American, American Becoming.* New York: Russell Sage, 1999.

Matthews, Glenna. *Silicon Valley, Women, and the California Dream: Gender, Class, and Opportunity in the Twentieth Century.* Stanford, Calif.: Stanford University Press, 2003.

Mauk, David. *The Colony That Rose from the Sea: Norwegian Maritime Migration in Brooklyn, 1850–1910*. Urbana: University of Illinois Press, 1998.

McEvoy, Arthur F. *The Fisherman's Problem: Ecology and Law in California Fisheries, 1850–1980*. Cambridge, U.K.: Cambridge University Press, 1986.

McGoodwin, James R. *Crisis in the World's Fisheries: People, Problems, Policies*. Stanford, Calif.: Stanford University Press, 1990.

———. *Understanding the Cultures of Fishing Communities: A Key to Fisheries Management and Food Security*. Rome: Food and Agriculture Organization of the United Nations, 2001.

McKibben, Carol. "The Women of the Canneries." *Alta Vista Magazine*, February 1991.

McWilliams, Carey. *California: The Great Exception*. Salt Lake City: Peregrine Books, 1979.

Miller, James. *Salt in the Blood: Scotland's Fishing Communities Past and Present*. Edinburgh: Canongate, 1995.

Moch, Leslie Page. *Moving Europeans: Migration in Western Europe since 1650*. Bloomington: Indiana University Press, 1992.

Monroy, Douglas. *Thrown among Strangers: The Making of Mexican Culture in Frontier California*. Berkeley: University of California Press, 1990.

Nokunas, Martha K. *The Politics of Public Memory: Tourism, History, and Ethnicity in Monterey, California*. Albany: State University of New York Press, 1993.

Nugent, Walter. *Crossings: The Great Transatlantic Migrations, 1870–1914*. Bloomington: Indiana University Press, 1992.

Orsi, Robert Anthony. *The Madonna of 115th Street: Faith and Community in Italian Harlem, 1880–1950*. New Haven, Conn.: Yale University Press, 1985.

Philbrick, Nathaniel. *In the Heart of the Sea: The Tragedy of the Whaleship Essex*. New York: Viking Penguin, 2000.

Pomeroy, Earl. *The Pacific Slope: A History of California, Oregon, Washington, Idaho, Utah, and Nevada*. Seattle: University of Washington Press, 1965.

Poggie, John J., and Richard B. Pollnac, eds. *Small-Scale Fishery Development: Socio-Cultural Perspectives*. Kingston, R.I.: International Center for Marine Resource Development, 1991.

Portes, Alejandro. "Immigration Theory for a New Century: Some Problems and Opportunities." *International Migration Review* 31 (winter 1997): 799–825.

———. "Transnational Communities: Their Emergence and Significance in the Contemporary World System." In *Latin America and the World Economy*, eds. R. P. Korzeniewidcz and W. C. Smith. Westport, Conn.: Greenwood Press, 1996.

Portes, Alejandro, and Ruben G. Rumbaut, eds. *Ethnicities: Children of Immigrants in America*. Berkeley: University of California Press, 2001.

———. *Immigrant America: A Portrait*. Berkeley: University of California Press, 1996.

Radin, Paul. *The Italians of San Francisco*. North Stratford, N.H.: Ayer Co. Publ., 1975.

Reeder, Linda. "Conflict across the Atlantic: Women, Family and Mass Male Migration in Sicily, 1880–1920." *IRSH* 46 (2001): 371–91.

———. "When the Men Left Sutera: Sicilian Women and Mass Migration, 1880–1920." In *Women, Gender, and Transnational Lives: Italian Workers of the World*, eds. Donna Gabaccia and Franca Iocovetta. Toronto: University of Toronto Press, 2002, 45–67.

Reinstadt, Randall. *Where Have All the Sardines Gone?: A Pictorial History of Cannery Row.* Pacific Grove, Calif.: Ghost Town Publications, 1978.

Rolle, Andrew. *The Immigrant Upraised: Italian Adventures and Colonists in an Expanding America.* Norman: University of Oklahoma Press, 1968.

———. *The Italian Americans: Troubled Roots.* New York: The Free Press, 1980.

Rosenberg, Emily S. *A Date Which Will Live: Pearl Harbor in American Memory.* Durham, N.C.: Duke University Press, 2003.

Ruiz, Vicki. *Cannery Women, Cannery Lives: Mexican Women, Unionization, and the California Food Processing Industry, 1930–1950.* Albuquerque: University of New Mexico Press, 1987.

Ryan, Mary. *Civic Wars: Democracy and Public Life in the American City during the Nineteenth Century.* Berkeley: University of California Press, 1998.

———. *Cradle of the Middle Class: The Family in Oneida County New York, 1790–1865.* Cambridge, U.K.: Cambridge University Press, 1981.

———. *Women in Public: Between Banners and Ballots, 1825–1880.* Baltimore and London: Johns Hopkins University Press, 1990.

Sassen, Saskia. *Losing Control? Sovereignty in an Age of Globalization.* New York: Columbia University Press, 1996.

Schneider, A. " 'Putting an Ocean between Them': Gender Relations among Italian Immigrant Families in Twentieth Century Argentina." *Immigrants and Minorities* 15, 3 (1996): 193–213.

Schneider, Jane, and Peter Schneider. *Culture and Political Economy in Western Sicily.* New York: Academic Press, 1976.

Schuck, Peter. *Citizens, Strangers and In-Betweens: Essays on Immigration and Citizenship.* Boulder, Colo.: Westview, 1998.

Simon, Rita James, and Caroline Brettell, eds. *International Migration: The Female Experience.* Totowa, N.J.: Rowman and Allanheld, 1986.

Smith, M. Estellie, ed. *Those Who Live from the Sea: A Study in Maritime Anthropology.* St. Paul, Minn.: West Publication Company, 1999.

Smith, Rogers M. *Civic Ideals: Conflicting Visions of Citizenship in U.S. History.* New Haven, Conn.: Yale University Press, 1997.

Spoehr, Alexander. *Maritime Adaptions: Essays on Contemporary Fishing.* Pittsburgh, Pa.: University of Pittsburgh Press, 1980.

Stack, Carol B. *All Our Kin: Strategies for Survival in a Black Community.* New York: Harper and Row, 1974.

Starr, Kevin. *Embattled Dreams: California in War and Peace, 1940–1950.* Oxford: Oxford University Press, 2002.

Steinbeck, John. *Cannery Row.* New York: Bantam Viking, 1945, 24–25.

Thernstrom, Stephan. *Poverty and Progress: Social Mobility in a Nineteenth Century City.* Cambridge, Mass.: Harvard University Press, 1964.

Thistlethwaite, Frank. "Migration from Europe Overseas in the Nineteeth and Twentieth Centuries." In *A Century of European Migration, 1830–1930,* eds. Rudolph J. Vecoli and Suzanne M. Sinke. Chicago: University of Chicago Press, 1991.

Tilly, Charles. "Migration in Modern European History." In *Human Migration,* eds. William H. McNeill and Ruth S. Adams. Bloomington: Indiana University Press, 1978.

Vecoli, Rudolph J. "The Contadini in Chicago: A Critique of the Uprooted." *Journal of American History* 51 (1964–65): 404–17.

———. "European Americans: From Immigrants to Ethnics." *International Migration Review* 6 (1972): 403–34.

Vecoli, Rudolph J., and Suzanne M. Sinke, eds. *A Century of European Migrations, 1830–1930.* Chicago: University of Chicago Press, 1991.

Walton, John. "Cannery Row: Class, Community, and the Social Construction of History." In *Reworking Class,* by John R. Hall. Ithaca, N.Y.: Cornell University Press, 1997.

———. *Storied Land: Community and Memory in Monterey.* Berkeley: University of California Press, 2001.

Yamada, David. *The Japanese of the Monterey Peninsula: The History and Legacy, 1895–1995.* Monterey, Calif.: Japanese American Citizens League, 1995.

Yans-McLaughlin, Virginia. *Family and Community: Italian Immigrants in Buffalo, 1880–1930.* Ithaca, N.Y.: Cornell University Press, 1977.

———. *Immigration Reconsidered: History, Sociology, and Politics.* New York: Oxford University Press, 1990.

Zavella, Patricia. *Women's Work and Chicano Families: Cannery Workers of the Santa Clara Valley.* Ithaca, N.Y.: Cornell University Press, 1987.

Zaya, Cynthia Neri. *The Ethnographies of Two Japanese Maritime Communities.* Quezon City, Philippines: Third World Studies Center, 1999.

Index

CAROL LYNN MCKIBBEN is a public historian and independent scholar in Monterey, California. She is currently the director of the Monterey Bay Regional Oral History and Immigration Project for the city of Monterey.

Statue of Liberty–Ellis Island Centennial Series

The University of Illinois Press
is a founding member of the
Association of American University Presses.

———————————————————————

University of Illinois Press
1325 South Oak Street
Champaign, IL 61820-6903
www.press.uillinois.edu